Praise for

KICKFLIP BOYS

"Watching Thompson come of age alongside his two rebellious boys was unexpectedly moving. *Kickflip Boys* is a relatable, warts-and-all story of a family sticking together and, once in a while, soaring alongside one another. Nobody in this memoir is perfect, which is what makes it so great."   —*Glamour* (Top 10 Books of 2018)

"[A] thoughtful, honest memoir of fathering two young sons who want nothing else but to immerse themselves in skateboard culture and everything (the graffiti, drugs, and more) that goes with it."
                    — *Outside* (Best Summer Books)

"Open-eyed. . . . [Thompson] shares his journey, and the journey of his family, with us in a heartfelt, vulnerable way that will resonate with any parent, but especially the parents of teenage boys."
                    —*Star Tribune* (Minneapolis)

"With a dispassionate but tender eye, Thompson captures the ache, fizz, yearning, and frustration of being the father of adolescent boys—and of adolescence itself, observed and remembered."
                    —Michael Chabon

"An honest account of raising creative, rebellious boys who happen to love skateboarding. Having been through the fire of raising a few free-thinking boys myself, I found *Kickflip Boys* to be fun, moving, raw, and relatable."   —Tony Hawk

"What a riveting, touching, and painful read! My stomach was in knots page after page. *Kickflip Boys* makes you think about parenting, nature vs. nurture, and how fast it all goes, the good times and the bad. I felt deeply for Thompson and his family throughout and was—and am—rooting for them."   —Maria Semple

KICKFLIP BOYS

ALSO BY NEAL THOMPSON

A Curious Man:
The Strange and Brilliant Life of Robert "Believe It or Not!" Ripley

Hurricane Season:
A Coach, His Team, and Their Triumph in the Time of Katrina

Driving with the Devil:
Southern Moonshine, Detroit Wheels, and the
Birth of NASCAR

Light This Candle:
The Life & Times of Alan Shepard, America's First Spaceman

ecco
An Imprint of HarperCollins*Publishers*

KICKFLIP BOYS

A MEMOIR OF FREEDOM,
REBELLION, AND THE
CHAOS OF FATHERHOOD

NEAL THOMPSON

HarperCollins books may be purchased for educational, business, or sales promotional use. For information, please e-mail the Special Markets Department at SPsales@harpercollins.com.

A hardcover edition of this book was published in 2018 by Ecco, an imprint of HarperCollins Publishers.

FIRST ECCO PAPERBACK EDITION PUBLISHED 2019.

Designed by Michelle Crowe
Background image by I. Friedrich/Shutterstock, Inc.
Spray paint texture by Tomash Sugint/Shutterstock, Inc.
Skateboard photograph by Mega Pixel/Shutterstock, Inc.
Chapter opener photographs are from the author's collection.

The Library of Congress has catalogued a previous edition as follows:

Names: Thompson, Neal, author.
Title: Kickflip boys : a memoir of freedom, rebellion, and the chaos of
    fatherhood / Neal Thompson.
Description: First edition. | New York, NY : Ecco, 2018.
Identifiers: LCCN 2017052651 | ISBN 9780062394347 (hardback)
Subjects: LCSH: Skateboarding—Social aspects—United States. |
Autonomy in
    adolescence. | Parenting. | Fathers and sons—United States—
Biography. |
    Thompson, Neil. | BISAC: BIOGRAPHY & AUTOBIOGRAPHY /
Personal Memoirs. |
    FAMILY & RELATIONSHIPS / Parenting / General. | BIOGRAPHY
& AUTOBIOGRAPHY
    / Sports.
Classification: LCC GV859.8 .T475 2018 | DDC 796.22—dc23 LC record
available at https://lccn.loc.gov/2017052651

ISBN 978-0-06-239436-1 (pbk.)
19 20 21 22 23   10 9 8 7 6 5 4 3 2 1

To my bold and beautiful boys,
my best friends, my heroes . . .
This is my attempt to celebrate
your big, bold lives.
To Mary, my partner in every adventure.

We did these things in darkness and in the light of day,
moving always to the sound of breaking glass and
yowling cats and grinding metal.

—Tobias Wolff, *This Boy's Life*

A father is a man who fails every day.

—Michael Chabon

AUTHOR'S NOTE

I spotted Tony Hawk sitting at a Lower East Side café, walked up, and introduced myself.

For years, I'd been trying to reach him, hoping that an interview with the world's most famous skater might reveal some insider information about who my boys were, and where they were headed. I told Hawk about my kids and the book I was trying to write, and he agreed to an interview. Weeks later, when we talked by phone, I asked him to help me understand the stage my wife and I found ourselves in, with two pathologically rebellious teen skaters on our hands, a stage that seemed to go on and on.

"Why are they drawn to the *fringe?*" I asked, knowing that

he had skate sons of his own. "Why the distrust of authority, the outsider attitude?"

What I really wondered: What are we doing wrong, and how can we fix it?

Hawk told me some kids—kids like him—craved an identity that differed from their peers, and skating gave it to them. I totally got that part. I'd *been* that kid. I just wondered when they might transition from skate life to *life* life. He agreed that skaters all faced that moment when they "take responsibility for yourself and become a member of society."

Some of them abide; some don't. "But your kids can always hold on to that sense of individuality," he said. "They need to just figure out a way to make that uniqueness work in their favor."

Their *uniqueness*. That's what I'd always cherished. For nearly a decade, skating had been something my kids did, alone or with friends, day and night, indoors and out, for two or four or six hours straight. Who does *anything* for six hours, except sleep and work?

Still, at times while writing this book, dragging myself and my family back to our roughest patches, I'd sometimes wonder (as would they), *Why?* Why dwell on my kids' noncompliant past? But the truth is: I loved those days. I've loved *all* of our days. I'd reached a point where I needed to relive those moments, to celebrate them, the good and the bad.

Though my wife worried that writing about our kids would "memorialize our incompetence," I lobbied that it would "celebrate our persistence." Probably a little of both.

Writing this book was as much an exercise in therapy as it was reportage and storytelling. And as I plunged deeper and began slowly admitting aloud that I was actually writing a skate dad memoir, I was frequently shocked at how many parents had stories to share. They had skate kids, or they'd been skaters, or they had a defiant, pot-smoking teen somewhere in the family.

We were hardly alone, I learned. That's what convinced me that our story, and theirs, was worth sharing. Despite all the risks.

I knew I was exposing my kids and my wife. After many uneasy discussions along the way, they agreed to come along for the ride, a profound act of generosity that humbled me. They read, they edited, they corrected me, scolded me, and did what they could to fix what needed fixing. For that, I'm eternally grateful and proud. But I should be clear: any fuck-ups are mine alone.

Like any memoir delving into the minefields of family history, this story required a delicate balance of revelation and obfuscation, involving a handful of bent rules, the kind I wasn't used to bending. As a journalist—and an ex-Catholic—I'm professionally, *physically* incapable of bullshitting. Yet for the sake of narrative flow, in a few instances similar scenes were merged, and the timing of a few scenes was tweaked. And since this story contains teen drug use, for the sake of college admissions—and any future political aspirations—I changed a couple names.

Beyond that, everything happened as described. At least as I remembered it.

KICKFLIP BOYS

PART 1
DROPPING IN

1

Until the grown-ups come to fetch us,
we'll have fun.

—William Golding, *Lord of the Flies*

FOOD LION SKATEPARK
ASHEVILLE, NC

There were fits and starts, but the real moment, at least for me, began when Leo nailed his first drop-in.

Clad in the protective plastic armor required by management—helmet, knee, elbow, and wrist pads—Leo stood at the rim of the concrete bowl, right foot on his kid-size board, waiting for an opening in the action. Half a dozen skaters were rolling in and around the U-shaped bowl, ranging from preteen to twenty-something to grandpa: a wobbly, pudgy, ponytailed old dude in a white tank top, happily swirling around the smooth surface like a golf ball dropped into a bathtub.

Leo had just turned eight and was determined to master the drop-in, one of skating's landmark accomplishments, like catching your first wave, slapping your first base hit. He'd lean forward, lift his back foot onto the board, and tilt into the concrete belly, trying to time his descent and avoid a collision. Yet on each attempt, as he tipped over the edge he'd jump off and chase his runaway board. The other skaters would skirt around him or his board, and I worried they'd start getting pissed at this cute but annoying little noob. Instead, I overheard their coaxing: "Nice try, kid" . . . "You can do it" . . . "Almost, dude." Even old ponytail weighed in with encouragement: "Try staying *forward*."

Leo tried and bailed, tried and bailed, and I forced myself not to intervene. But I also realized he wasn't actually bothering the other skaters. Despite his size and hesitance, he was one of them—or was about to be. The scene was so different from the baseball or soccer fields of his and Sean's halfhearted forays into team sports, where typically only the best kids got to play. Here, amid the whoosh and thwack of polyurethane wheels on wave-shaped concrete, amid the shouts and laughs of boys, young men, and one lone girl, there were no jacked-up parents cheering or jeering at coaches and refs. Here, Leo's coaches, refs, and teammates were his fellow skaters. And they were all pulling for him.

I realized something else as I sat at a picnic table, drinking coffee and pretending to read a magazine, our big white dog curled at my feet . . . Leo wasn't on the sidelines or in the dugout waiting for the call-up. He wasn't on JV hoping for a shot at varsity. I wasn't stressed about whether he'd get a base hit or a foot on the soccer ball. He was out there in a muddle of skaters, all ages and skill levels, smaller than the rest but doing his best, trying the same maneuver again and again, which was enough to earn a spot in the mix.

After more than a dozen attempts, Leo pushed over the rim, leaned forward, rolled down the slope and kept both feet glued to his board. Arms wide for balance, he rolled up the other side, kick-turned and rolled back in. The other skaters circled in close, buzzed past him, and then . . . they clapped, or patted his back, or gave his helmet a tap. They said "yeah" or "nice!" or "good job." One kid slapped his board against the lip of the bowl, which I'd learn was a skater's form of applause. They didn't make too huge a deal of it. It was subtle enough. But they'd all been watching as another tyke strived to join their club, as he achieved the feeling—of what, freedom? *flight?*—that they'd felt their first time.

Leo tried to play it cool, nodded his thanks, tamped down his smile. And Dad? A quick-to-cry softy, I had to turn away and hide my melty face behind my *New Yorker*.

Years later, I'd still get teary over the memory of that transitional day, long before my boys and their skating would bring me to tears for other reasons.

Leo's inaugural drop-in wasn't quite my introduction to skaters and skate parks. He and Sean—a year and a half older, now nine—had been skateboarding on and off for more than a year, and I'd been taking them on occasional skate outings. But like an anthropologist witnessing some tribal ritual in the wild, it was my first unfiltered exposure to the unexpected nurturing, the antithetical and empathetic embrace, of the culture of the board.

Don't get me wrong. It's not like the skate scene welcomed eight-year-olds with hugs and cookies. Like surfing and snow-boarding, there was a rite-of-passage aspect to gaining entry into the club. If it'd been me trying to drop in, old ponytail might've elbowed me in the neck. But it's not like there was a skater's checklist, either. It was more about attitude. And whatever it was skaters looked for, Leo had it. Sean did, too, having graduated from Food Lion's beginner bowl to the more challenging street-skating section, whose patrons were more tattooed and intense, no grandpas or toddlers.

This interest in skating was in stark contrast to their attempts at traditional sports. I treasure my shaky videos of Sean digging for worms in right field or throwing his mitt in the air as baseballs rolled past. Leo tried baseball (not bad, but not for him), then some soccer (pretty good, actually—he was *fast*), and later, somewhat bravely, basketball (surprisingly good, despite being the smallest kid on every team). Mary and I dutifully drove them to practices and games, encouraged their largely ho-hum efforts, whipped out the video camera when they got to play, displayed their framed team photos on a shelf. Yet, for all of us there seemed to be something missing, some spark that failed to ignite.

When skateboarding beckoned—a nightingale's song? a siren's song?—my kids found their tribe. Before we knew it, they were both pulled deeply into the skate scene, as were Mary and I, practically swept off our feet by this balletic sport and its eccentric cast of players. Much of what I came to appreciate about skating had been on display that day Leo dropped in. Namely: skating is hard, it takes lots of practice, it requires patience, persistence, self-reliance, and guts. It develops mechanical and navigational skills, social and negotiating skills, an ability to converse and collaborate with strangers young and old, while avoiding the creepers and the pushers who seem to lurk near skate parks. With no real rules, skaters had to be creative, innovative, imaginative. And they had to assimilate into a community that distrusted assimilation.

My boys met other skaters who were refreshingly familiar. Smart kids with a bit of attitude. Curious kids with a disregard for convention. They dressed semisloppily but with bits of flair—shoelace belts and skate-logo T shirts, beanies or snap-back sports caps, skinny jeans or cutoffs. They listened to rap and hip-hop, whose slang and profanity became theirs. Some of the older skaters sported tattoos or earrings, dreadlocks, green hair, or a Mohawk.

What surprised me during those early days was just how polite and nice those raggedy skaters seemed. The badass outer shell some wore like armor—smoking or drinking at a skate park, for example, which we *didn't* witness on the ball fields—wasn't always matched by skater stereotypes: no pissed-off thugs, reckless ravers, or dumb-ass dropouts. It sometimes seemed as if my kids had revealed to us the secret truths about some misunderstood subculture, as if discovering that the Hells Angels knitted and played Scrabble.

Despite a few hard edges, or maybe because of them, my boys seemed more at ease among sloppy-slouchy skaters than with their more earnest T-ball teammates. So did I, happy to spend a few hours at a skate park with my laptop, a notebook, a coffee, a book, the dog. I'd sit at a picnic table, watching them practice or just leaving them alone, giving them their space as I wrote or read or walked the dog.

Mostly—since there wasn't a coach to ask "how're they doing?"—I hovered at the edges, a voyeur. I didn't try to join them or coach them. I let them discover skating at their own pace. Leo quickly became the bolder one, drawn to the bowls in the "vert" section, while Sean preferred the technical precision (and outlaw hint) of the flat-ground "street" section. In time, they'd both gravitate—for reasons that'd only later become obvious to me—toward the urban, off-limits aura of the style known as *street skating*.

A t the start, Mary and I were totally, Kool-Aid-drinking on board. Maybe even a little relieved. It was a culture that meshed nicely with our own sensibilities. We were fine not spending weeknights and weekends alongside other parents in bleachers or on sidelines. We were comfortable in our roles as mostly hands-off skate parents.

We loved that they were outdoors and active, day after day. They'd skate for hours, getting sweaty and sunburned, stopping to gulp Gatorade and chips. Between bouts of skating, Sean and Leo would cluster with other skaters, asking about their "setup" (board, trucks, wheels), or their shoes, or their tricks. I was intrigued by all the nonverbal negotiations. Who rolls first into a bowl? All it took was a nod of a head. My board hit your shin? A shrug served as an apology. Nail a trick? The tapping of a board was your applause.

There was always someone a little better, or a lot better, and I'd see the boys studying the good skaters, taking mental notes. I once nervously watched Sean stand at the lip of a steep bowl for what seemed like ten full minutes, at the edge of the action as other skaters dropped in beside and beneath him. Sean then turned and walked off without dropping in. When I asked him about it, he shrugged. "Just watching."

As a team sports alum—baseball, football, and track, always solidly mediocre, until I discovered my own boards, waterskiing and, especially, skiing—I'd never witnessed a sport without hierarchy: coaches and refs, varsity and JV, starters and bench warmers. Skaters taught themselves, coached themselves, policed themselves. They never had to wait for an authority figure to give them *permission* to play. The skate park was a communal playground, almost familial: we're in this together, a league of outcasts, let's all just get along!

As a work-at-home writer, I had the flexibility to drive them to and from skate parks. That put me on the front line, as observer and facilitator. Encouraged by their passion, I pushed them to explore skating to its fullest. Later, I'd discover that not every park was as mellow as Food Lion Skatepark, not every skater a misunderstood angel.

My initial view had been hopeful, a bit narrow, even a bit clueless. In fact, before we knew it, our sons were pushing beyond the cute introductory phase into the darker corners of skate culture. That beckoning, that exploration of the shadowy side . . . turns out that was skateboarding, too. By then, there was no turning back. I'd find myself wishing I could've cornered that old guy from Food Lion, grabbed his ponytail, and asked, *Why didn't you* warn *me?*

And later, when I wondered how and why things got so fucking messy and hard, I'd imagine the old guy's laughing response: *Dude, you steered them right into it.*

Leo's drop-in at Food Lion marked the start of my soon-to-be-complicated role as a skate dad. I watched as my kids joined a subset of postmillennial boys for whom skating represented more than a hobby or sport; it was an articulation of who they were, and who they weren't. They were smart boys with sporadic interest in academics, seemingly allergic to conventional expectations. They were part of a growing demographic: distracted, disenfranchised, bored. They were drawn to the whiff of outlaw, the sounds of gangsta rap, and eventually the stink of weed. And they all shared two maddening traits: noncompliance and its angrier cousin, defiance.

From their first steps, their earliest words, both boys strived to navigate the world on their own often intractable terms. They wanted to have fun. They didn't understand the point of so many rules. They didn't respect boundaries. They considered themselves outside the herd. They cherished the words *no* and *why* and *why not*. Skateboarding—a sport built on defying grown-ups, defying mainstream mores, defying gravity, fear, prudence, safety—helped them define their terms, and would stoke the battles to come.

On the parenting spectrum, Mary and I fell somewhere left of the dial, in a loose-leashed zone of liberal boundaries and tolerance. We walked a fine line, though—or tried to. We loved them dearly, fiercely. But we decided early on that we'd stay out of their way, much as our parents had. We'd let them explore and be free, shooing them into the world but preventing them from veering too far. We'd be willing to let them fail. And we'd soon find ourselves tolerating everyday misdeeds that'd give a hard-core Tiger Mom a stroke.

We had no idea that by opening the door to skate-rat culture that we'd invited something wild into our home, as if Jeff Spicoli, Sean Penn's surfer-skater-stoner dude from *Fast Times at Ridgemont High*, came for dinner and never left. Spicoli would become the devilish voice whispering in my kids' ears: "Hey, Bud, let's party!"

The story of raising sons, especially willful challengers of authority, is universal, it's *biblical*. So's the lure of the dark side. Everyone knows a teen rebel, and/or they were one themselves. Some parents tighten their grip, keep their kids close, pack their schedule with violin lessons and drama club and other building blocks to an impressive college application. Others, either by choice or resignation, give their kids the space and freedom they demand, and hope they find their own way.

When I first started writing about my kids and their skating, I envisioned a story about the gnarly history of an American-born sport that became a refuge for boys like mine. But over time I found my gaze turning inward, the journalist that I'd once been taking over, aiming questions at myself. Have I been a good father? Have I ignored the danger signs? Am I the one who welcomed Spicoli and Co. into our lives? Have I given my boys too long a leash? And why didn't I anticipate that they'd exploit it? Just as I had.

Then again, I wasn't alone. I'd chosen a like-minded partner, someone as impetuous and rootless as me, someone who thrived on a bit of disruption, even a bit of chaos, who wrestled with the same parental questions: How do you raise unconventional, freedom-seeking kids to be self-reliant but obedient, happy but successful, good but free, free but safe? Throughout all the battles to come, it'd be us against them, and them against the world. This is a story of survival. Theirs, and ours.

2

I first fell for her walk.

Watching her hike ahead of me, up a mountain trail in southwest Virginia, all chinos and a tank top . . . I fell for her stride, her confidence, her irreverence, her runner's build, her New York-y style. I thought: this is someone who knows who she is, where she wants to go, how she wants to get there, but is game for why-not diversions.

Mary had come to visit her sister, a colleague at the newspaper where I worked. Mary and I flirted as we hiked, and I invited her to my apartment for dinner, then burned chicken on a grill. We kissed that night while walking through Mini Graceland, the decorated yard of an obsessive Elvis fan's homage. I visited her in New York, where she produced TV commercials. When I moved to Florida she came for a long weekend and we drank beers and got stoned at a drive-in beside an orange processing plant, car windows open, the air sweetly orangey, watching Jean-Claude Van Damme kick some ass—and I fell hard. Months later, I awoke to find the Gulf of Mexico knee high in my house, then chest high, as an unnamed winter storm swamped the coast that Saturday morning. I smashed out a kitchen window, watched my Subaru bob and float, and the first person I called was Mary. Within weeks, I'd loaded the handful of my nonflooded possessions into an insurance-paid pickup and moved to New York, much sooner than she had likely expected.

Also much sooner than she had anticipated, I told her I loved her—at a Holiday Inn beside a New Jersey Turnpike exit. This was after a friend's wedding, and I was inspired by the image of her bending over a pool table to make a shot. Her response to my "I love you" was "thank you."

She didn't flinch when I bought a lovable but impractical twenty-five-year-old BMW 2002, a speedy thing we named "Buddy" that I drove like a weapon. She flinched a little when I asked her to move in together, and then to pay for my overdue student loan one month. And then the next. She was fit and funny, mischievous and curious; a smart-ass with a gymnast's physique. We skied, ran, hiked, and biked; we loved to drink and play. Both lapsed Catholics and rule benders, we'd sneak beers into a theater and stick around for a free double feature.

Six months after my move to New York, we spent a weekend on eastern Long Island, and while walking through the Montauk sand dunes, regrettably without a ring, I proposed. A decade later, we had moved from New York to New Jersey (where Sean was born) to Maryland (where Leo was born). While our friends settled into their first homes, building equity and sink-ing roots, we bought and sold two fixer-uppers, then landed in North Carolina, nursing another old house back from disrepair.

We'd both signed on for a mobile, malleable life, a life of "why nots," a life on our terms. If I recall, the decision to leave New York and buy our first house, while on tour with a new Jersey realtor, had consisted of a raised eyebrow, *Well?*, and a shrug, *Sure!* We were proudly nimble. "We're like cats," Mary once said. "We always land on our feet."

Our life together, ten years so far, had already been a zig-zaggy series of bold and borderline impulsive decisions that, to friends and family, must've seemed random or reckless.

And we were just warming up.

Our latest move—in 2002, from suburban Baltimore to hippy, arty, vegan, boozy Asheville, nestled in the folds of the Blue Ridge and Smoky Mountains—came partly in response to 9/11. Like many families, we found ourselves in a reboot after the terrorist attacks, asking: Where should we be right now? Where will our children be safe?

Mary had been working for a film company in D.C. at the time, and was driving toward her office when the first plane hit the first tower. I'd been scheduled to give a talk to a group of navy veterans (prompted by the book I'd begun researching, a biography of the astronaut Alan Shepard) at a luncheon near the Pentagon. I called Mary, catching her halfway to D.C., and she circled back, and together we watched the tragedy unfold on CNN, crying and praying that none of our New York friends were among the victims.

During those sober September days, Sean insisted on wearing what he called his "worker guy" outfit—dress shirt, bow tie, blazer—around the house, in the backyard, and to school. Leo became obsessed with the Grinch. He'd watch the Jim Carrey movie repeatedly and at bedtime made us read the Seuss book a half dozen times before he'd go to sleep. At dinner one night, Sean asked if he could say a prayer . . . Mary and I exchanged looks—we hadn't done much praying as a family.

Sean theatrically lowered his head and led us: "God is gracious. Thanks for our food. Oh-*man*."

Oh, man.

Mary and I had our own erratic reactions to 9/11. Six weeks later, we decided not to cancel a long-planned trip to Ireland. (I'd recently become a naturalized Irish citizen.) Tucked inside cozy Dublin pubs I thought: Let's live here! Back in Baltimore, we talked of returning to New York, to the place where we'd married at a cathedral high above the Hudson River. But then we pivoted and started looking in the other direction, to the south, far from the terrorist targets of the Northeast.

We chose Asheville partly to be near the research for a book I'd started writing (about southern moonshiners and the roots of NASCAR). The other draw was Mary's parents, who lived outside Asheville. In the 9/11 aftermath, raising our boys near Grandpa Bill and Grandma Pauline felt right, no matter how wacky our move would later seem.

The day we pulled away from our perfectly remodeled and manicured Baltimore home, the boys were downright giddy.

"*Well!*" gushed Sean. "Here we go, off on another one of those wild goose bumps."

We fell quickly, madly for the town *Rolling Stone* once dubbed "Freakville, U.S.A."

Asheville was scruffy and outdoorsy, proud of its weirdness, a culture that championed coffee and beer, music and books. I loved the freaky Friday night drum circle, the impromptu fiddle jams outside Malaprop's Bookstore, the mottled mix of rednecks and trustafarians, writers and retirees. And I loved that it was ours: *we* had chosen *it*, not some employer or job. For the first year, it seemed like we'd gotten away with something: *Did we really pull this off?*

Unlike me, happily alone at libraries and coffee shops with my new book project, Mary was diligently social and quickly befriended other moms with young kids. The boys made playground buddies, and the dads became my friends.

One summer night, two of the dads came over, their three boys in tow, to help me rebuild our sagging garage. The kids climbed on the lumber stacked in the driveway, scrambled over bags of cement mix, dug into piles of sand and gravel. Mary was at work, and she and the other moms would arrive soon for a barbecue. Until then, the evening was messy and male. It smelled of sawn wood and power tools, then lighter fluid, charcoal, and beer, accompanied by the twangs of Dick Dale surf music. A swampy southern evening.

Leo and Sean, now five and six, were playing in the front yard with the other boys while Eric, John, and I finished our work and drank our beers and prepped the grill.

Then a red ball rolled down the driveway, and into the street.

The boys hovered at the edge, daring one another to get it.

Sean, the eldest, stepped into the road.

The driver, who lived in a nearby apartment complex, was traveling thirty miles an hour in her Corolla; thirty in a fifteen-mile-an-hour zone; thirty past the yellow sign that read SLOW CHILDREN PLAYING; thirty miles an hour . . . while *texting*. We heard the thud of impact, the screech of tires, and the driver's screams. In that order. Thud. Screech. Scream. In an instant, Sean was airborne, cartwheeling an arc through the summer sky, the other boys watching in confused horror, their mouths just opening into howls.

Manning the grill, I had my back to the street and saw nothing. Eric, who looked over my shoulder in time to see Sean midflight, later told me his first emotion was anger: "Why the fuck is he flying? Boys don't *fly*." I can still picture Eric's bugged-out eyes, just before he dropped his beer can and ran. I followed in a panic and found Sean crumpled in a terrible heap on our neighbor's front lawn. His body was all wrong—left leg bent midthigh and twisted, foot up by his ear, eyes shut. Afraid to touch him, I clawed at the grass and dirt, animal screams howling out from someplace deep inside. For the worst minute of my life, I thought—no, I just *knew*—my boy was dead.

John ran up yelling, "Where's the phone, the *phone*, I can't find the phone!" Eric, all war-zone cool, reached across Sean's body and grabbed me by the shoulders and shouted in my face, "You have to find it. Do it now. Go." I wrenched myself from Sean and ran crazily toward the house.

And there was Leo, screaming with the other shrieking kids and holding up his arms, *pleading* for comfort, his face red and contorted. But I pushed past him and into the house, found the phone, dialed 911 while sprinting back toward Sean, fully expecting to find that he'd breathed his last while I was gone . . .

As I dropped beside him, Sean's eyes fluttered and popped open. He was scared, foggy, but *awake*. An EMT was suddenly at my side, tugging me out of the way, taking control.

At the hospital, they stabilized Sean, and Mary finally arrived from work. (More war-zone cool: John's wife, Dana, had delivered the news with aplomb: "Mary? Don't worry, Sean's okay. He broke his leg. But . . . can you come to the hospital?") Once my in-laws and a couple friends showed up, and the adrenaline drained out of me, I locked myself in a bright-white bathroom, saw my stricken face in the mirror, and dropped to the floor, where I lay sobbing for five minutes. I'd never get those awful sounds out of my head: thud, screech, scream, fucking Dick Dale . . .

I had experienced every parent's worst nightmare. Except it wasn't the full nightmare. My boy had *survived*.

I had survived, too, I suppose. But something changed in me that day. Some innocent piece got gouged out and replaced by a lump of dread that pulses in my chest to this day.

I'd hardly been restrained as a kid, nor as a teen or young adult. I was a cautious daredevil—skateboarder, skier, water-skier, motorcycle rider, partier—and, frequently, a happy-go-lucky "don't worry about it" dumb ass. Not quite the heedless risk taker my younger brother had been, but still, no scaredy-cat. When Sean and Leo were born—less than two years apart, just like my brother and me—I didn't fret over their safety. I wanted to raise them to explore, to take chances, to *live*. But after Sean's accident, I fixated on their fragility. Obsessed with the speed of Sean's assaulter, I'd drive down our street trying to imagine slamming into a child. At night, I'd kneel beside the spot where Sean had landed, and I'd try to pray the old prayers I had learned in Catholic school, forgetting the words, hoping that my loony neighbor didn't come out and find me crying on her lawn.

I kept asking myself, *What have I done?* With Sean in traction, in a druggy fuddle? With Mary bleary-eyed beside his hospital bed? With a cocky young doctor wearing a blue blazer over his scrubs telling us Sean would need a cast from ankle to chest, that he might have lifelong back problems? I suddenly regretted the move south, the new house—it all seemed idiotic. *We almost lost one of our boys!* What kind of negligent father lets his kid chase a ball into the street? As a reporter, I'd written that child-hit-by-car story more than once, and I'd think: Where were the parents? Well . . . where was I? Drinking beer, listening to surf music—music that would forever remind me of my life's worst day.

Though I'd spent only a few hours at a hospital for my own injuries—severed fingertip after waterskiing, broken hand from a badly fought fight—I'd visited my wildman brother a few times: motorcycle accidents, a skimobile accident, his infamous forty-foot fall off a ski lift. The worst hospital visits had been for my mom (head injury after I graduated college) and my sister (a stroke a year after Mary and I got married).

Sitting beside Sean's bed, I desperately wished I could talk with my mom or sister, hold their hands, hug them.

Or at least laugh with them about what a terrible patient Sean was, sometimes hilariously so.

"Is this some kind of *joke?*" he'd yell, when his leg, locked in its traction device, ached and itched. Like a cranky old man, he'd shout to the nurses, "Somebody get in here and *fix* this." To the cocky ER doc in the blazer, he'd complain, "You don't know what it's *like!*" Had he told the doctor to shove a stethoscope up his ass, I would not have blinked.

Though the ER doctor warned that Sean might need to spend months in a half-body cast, a doctor friend helped us find a well-respected orthopedic surgeon, with the reassuringly biblical name of Moses, who told us there was no need for the body cast. "That's how we *used* to do things," he said with authority. Instead, he wanted to operate immediately. The procedure, inserting two foot-long pins called "femoral IM nails" into Sean's shattered thighbone, took two hours, and Moses came out drenched in sweat.

When I finally asked Sean to describe what he remembered about the accident, he told me he'd looked both ways, walked into the street, picked up the ball, then saw the car coming and assumed it would stop. When it didn't, he tried to jump. The EMTs told me the momentum from his half jump likely saved his life. After bouncing off the hood, Sean flew at an angle, into the neighbor's yard instead of straight onto the pavement, where a head injury might've killed him.

Sean remembered flying. And he remembered dying, just briefly. He described a white light, following it, then stopping and turning back. But first, there was an old man . . . "He had white hair. He was nice," Sean said. "I wasn't afraid."

Leo, meanwhile, would be haunted by what he saw. Years later, I'd find the brave three-page school essay he wrote about that day, a portion of which . . .

"He's dead. My one and only brother is dead. . . . They put him on a stretcher and took him away. And I stood on the porch. Alone."

In the hazy days that followed, Mary and I found ourselves mulling yet another big change, a reactionary pivot. As usual, we were in sync in our impetuousness.

The day Sean was released from the hospital, we all went for a drive. Winding along a pretty country road, Sean's wheelchair in the back, we passed a FOR SALE sign: LIVE IN THE BLUE RIDGE MOUNTAINS. 2.5 BEAUTIFUL ACRES WITH VIEWS. Mary and I exchanged looks—*Well?*—found the house, knocked on the door, got a tour from the owner. Wheeling Sean around the property, past gardens and fruit trees, watching Leo scamper across a green-carpet lawn, I thought: this is it. *This* is where we'll keep our children safe.

We sold the tainted downtown house and relocated our boys yet again—the fourth time in six years—setting in motion a whole new trajectory.

3

I n our pastoral new Appalachian home, surrounded by orchards, sunflower fields, tobacco farms, grazing cattle, and in the distance the blue-tinged mountains, we regrouped and recovered. We called it Happy Acres.

The shock of Sean's accident mellowed as we coaxed our fruits and vegetables, slept to the nightly peeps of tree frogs, awoke to the backyard strut of a wild turkey parade. Downtown Asheville had been lively, liberal, and liquored up. Twenty minutes north was a different scene altogether: farms and churches, tractors and pickup trucks, the occasional Confederate flag. It was also stunning and soothing, the light filtering through foggy-dewy mornings, exploding like fireworks at dusk.

Sean swapped his wheelchair for crutches. The leg brace came off and he started walking again, limping like a champ through painful physical therapy sessions. Six months after the accident, Sean had surgery again, to extract the titanium pins, which doctor Moses handed to us afterward inside a Ziploc. I thought about framing them, or burying them in our ex-neighbor's lawn, or making matching bracelets for Mary and me . . . but I knew I was just being dramatic. A week later, Moses assured us that Sean's leg had healed nicely and he was "free to go." It seemed way too soon for Sean to start running and jumping, I said, but Moses insisted, "Mr. Thompson, just let him be a boy again."

Leo and Sean went full-on country. They grew long hair, attended 4-H camp. Their country-kid wildlife checklist included bobcats, coyotes, bears, turkeys, deer, and foxes. They jumped into icy swimming holes, splashed in mountain streams, hunted for salamanders. They fished in Mary's parents' trout pond and watched Grandpa Bill kill copperheads with a shovel. Sean got a pet snake that he named, accurately enough, Snakey, who'd escape and turn up weeks later in a sock drawer or under a pillow.

With no cable TV or video games in our home, they learned to entertain themselves, to play and play hard. They loved fantasy games, mock battles and epic duels fought with sticks and plastic swords. They dressed in skintight Power Ranger and Batman costumes, crafted outfits of capes, wigs, and masks pulled from an overstuffed costume bin. More than anything, they loved to pound the piss out of each other, wrestling like WWF fighters, usually until someone got hurt and started bawling.

They didn't quite turn into woodland explorers, even with hiking trails out our back door. I'd try to shoo them up into the hills, but they rarely got far. So I built a backyard play-house on stilts, then a jungle gym, and a zip line, then bought a trampoline, where they'd bounce and tussle for hours. We got a giant white dog from a goat farm (defiantly untrain-able, as it turned out), and in our sprawling backyard they chased their dog and each other, fighting like the bear cubs we once saw wrestling on the nearby Blue Ridge Parkway, with mama bear looking on with an eye roll.

My boys . . . They were happy, and they were loved. They were funny, clever, naughty, sarcastic—a little cynical, a little weird. They were *boys*.

Leo: Silly, social, kind. Precociously articulate. Eager to please, easy to please. A blond, huggable optimist. "It'd be bad if the whole world was pavement. But it'd be cool if the whole world was trampoline." The sensitive one. Mourning our dead cat: "I wish nobody ever died. I wish there were no robbers. I wish the whole world was Hawaii."

Sean: Thoughtful, curious, passionate. Precociously ar-gumentative. Hard to read, hard to reach. A moody, serial questioner. "How can there be only one god? We're only a tiny planet." The combative one. After getting put into time-out: "I don't want to live with you anymore. I don't want a mommy, a daddy, a brother, *or* a government."

One day Sean came home from school complaining about his third grade teacher's thick drawl and southernisms: *ain't, cain't, y'all, you'uns*, etc. "She doesn't even speak proper English," he said. "How can she even be *teaching*?" He declared that he was now a *non-contractionist*: "I do not use words like *I'll* and *we'll*. I use words like *I will* and *we will*."

At the same time, he announced that he was a Buddhist and a vegetarian. He would spend the next two years religiously avoiding meat, except for fish.

"I don't think it's right to slaughter something that can grow up and have a good life," he once told us. "But fish? They don't really have a life."

We learned our son was becoming a nonconformist, too. His teacher called to tell us Sean was refusing to do assignments, putting his head down on the desk during reading time. We'd seen this side of him before. Back in Baltimore, his prekindergarten teacher had shared her concerns about Sean's disinterest in group activities, his preference for playing alone, his restlessness, and what she described in a note home as his "inflexibility and unwillingness to compromise."

"He does not accept discipline without a struggle and can be very stubborn and argumentative," the pre-K teacher had written. At the time, Mary and I were concerned and, simultaneously, proud. Now, four years later, his stubbornness flared anew, and his teacher requested a conference. She told us that Sean's refusal to do class work made him ineligible for the advanced-level English class, which infuriated Mary. "He just seems so smart and articulate," Mary said on the drive home. "I just don't *get* it."

Part of our parental frustration was: we kinda saw Sean's point. His teacher was very *country* (my euphemism for hillbilly) and hardly an inspiring educator. So . . . in the first of many such educational pivots, we decided that if Sean wasn't being challenged—and, in turn, Leo might not be either—we should find a school that was a better fit.

Looking back, we could have forced Sean to stay put and adapt. Instead, we transferred both boys to a shabby-chic charter school called Artspace. There, they befriended other hippie-country kids named Bear, River, Sequoia, Lorax, Lyric, Zyan, Zena, and Zander. The boys painted and made pottery, performed in school plays, dressed in costumes, and recited poetry. The Artspace vibe stressed self-reliance, self-expression, and nonjudgmental creativity. Artspace taught them: we're a little different, and so are you.

Something about that mix of freedom and creativity and "be yourself," I came to believe, contributed to their discovery of skateboarding.

Soon after our move to Asheville, Mary had gotten the boys a blue "Hobie da Cat" skateboard from Target, with the incongruous graphic of a cat on a snowboard, upside-down in midflip. On the sidewalk outside our short-term apartment complex, Sean and Leo had taken their first turns as skaters. At first they just stood on the board and popped wheelies. Attempts at motion ended in a tumble after hitting a pebble or a rut. As they gained confidence, they began taking small chances, skating off the curb, into the cul-de-sac, a few feet at a time, finding their balance. Sean would knock Leo off and grab the board. Leo would scream "I had it first, Sean!" then tackle his brother. And so on, until the tears.

When we moved into our fixer-upper house, atop a steep driveway, there was no place to skate. So the board got propped in a corner of the garage.

When we moved out to the country, even with all that open space, there was still no place to skate. The blue skateboard sat in that garage, too.

With more cows than kids nearby, it wasn't always easy watching them struggle to entertain themselves. I tried to help them find a hobby that might inspire. Having learned to play guitar at a young age, in church and in a high school band (The Vandals!), I felt responsible for exposing them to music. They cycled through violin, piano, flute, trumpet, guitar, and drums, but the lessons never lasted. I tried to teach them to ski, but they complained about my instructions—"I can do it myself!"—and kvetched that they'd rather be snowboarding. Except for Sean's interest in tennis—and, briefly, ballet—any activity requiring an instructor seemed doomed, as did my attempts at being their coach.

Then, while visiting my parents in Florida—including somber afternoons at the nursing home with my mother, who in her late sixties was suffering from dementia—Sean and Leo met two brothers skateboarding outside the condo. Each day the four boys met to skate, taking turns on the brothers' boards, and by week's end Sean and Leo had learned about the best skate companies, the best pro skaters, which companies sponsored which pro skaters. Those Florida kids opened a door and invited my sons inside.

"I was fascinated," Sean later told me.

Back home, they dug their Hobie da Cat board out of the garage and tried skating on our wooden back porch. Just as suddenly, Leo scorned it as "not a real skateboard."

"It's a board, with four wheels, how is it not a *skateboard?*" I tried, eliciting snorts. They had learned from their Florida pals that real boards didn't come from Target.

It took minimal prompting for us to buy them each a skateboard, which they'd forever remember as if remembering a first kiss. We spent an hour at an Asheville skate shop, where a cheerful, tattooed skater helped Sean select a paisley-patterned deck—a "shop deck," meaning it came with the shop's imprimatur and logo—trucks by Independent, wheels by Spitfire. The sales guy assembled it and affixed sandpapery grip tape, atop which Sean would later spray-paint "Yo," his first graffiti tag. Leo picked a preassembled setup from World Industries. (Skate speak: a skateboard, the board itself, is a "deck"; a full setup, with wheels and "trucks"—the front and rear axles—is a "complete.")

We bought helmets and, despite their protests, wrist and knee pads. I kept their gear in a mesh bag in the back of my truck—a red Toyota purchased on a whim, based partly on the seller's literary name: Thomas Wolfe—and in time we'd accumulate dozens of multicolored pieces that, like socks, seemed to constantly lose their mates. Mary and I drove them to Food Lion Skatepark, Zero Gravity Skate Park, to a weeklong summer skate camp. They removed Hobie da Cat's wheels and trucks and used that deck to practice tricks on the trampoline, bouncing and spinning it in midair. They amassed dozens of miniature fingerboards, using two fingers to "skate" them around the house, in sinks and tubs, flicking them off walls, furniture, and each other. Those sounds— ticka-tacka, chicka-chick, SCHWACK—it was as if wheeled cockroaches had infested our home.

Next they discovered the world of YouTube skate videos. If Mary or I complained about the YouTube noise, or the mixing bowls and cookbooks stacked to create a fingerboard obstacle course, or the broken fingerboard pieces we'd find under chairs and behind sofa pillows, their response was, *Take me to the skate park.*

So we did. And so it began.

It's hard to understate how relieved I was to see my kids— now nine and ten—finally find a passion. So much so that I decided to build a mini skate park of our own.

We paved our gravel driveway, and I made sure the crew created a wide, flat area at the bottom. Then I started building shit. At first it was just two-by-fours nailed together, so the boys had something to jump over and practice the rolling hop called an *ollie*. I bought orange cones for a slalom course, plywood for ramps, steel tubes that the boys dubbed "pee rails." With help off the Internet I graduated to building a wedge-shaped "kicker" ramp, a wooden box called a "mani-pad," and a rectangular box edged with metal "coping" for the boys to ollie onto and "grind" along. (Skate speak: a wheelie is a "manual"; a box atop which skaters perform manuals is a manual pad or mani-pad.)

A mess of lumber and metal accumulated at the bottom of our driveway, and as the boys improved we stoked their fervor. We subscribed to *Thrasher* and *Skateboarding* magazines. We bought T-shirts, shoes, and hats sporting skate company logos. Then, because there was only so much skating to be done in Asheville, we planned a skate-themed road trip.

In Washington, D.C., we visited our friends Lou and Tina, whose son Niall, born a week after Sean, had also become a devout skater. I made my first-ever skate videos on that trip with a recently purchased digital video camera. At Wakefield Skate Park, I ran around filming Sean, Leo, and Niall trading tricks and wipeouts. I also filmed Lou—like me, a former teen skater—doing old-school tricks on Niall's board. Lou told me how Niall now practiced ollies on their sidewalk for hours at a time, well past dark.

"Dude is *obsessed*," Lou said, and I told him my kids had caught the same fever.

We continued north to Philly to visit the renegade FDR park built by skaters beneath an Interstate 95 overpass. Mine were the only two kids wearing helmets. While carefully trying to drop down a steep ramp, Sean nearly got clobbered by an aggressive skater clearly sending him—and me—a message. Then Leo got trapped in a deep, graffiti-covered bowl, and I had to pull him out. Mary, who often exercised when nervous or bored, did squats as I shot more video. We stuck out like nerdy tourists.

That night we walked around Love Park, a public plaza across from Philly's City Hall whose granite ledges and stairs had been a skate mecca in the '80s and '90s. We didn't bring the boards because the park was now off-limits to skating. I later read that the park's creator—the father of actor Kevin Bacon—was furious over the ban. "I'd rather see them on a skateboard than running around trying to stab somebody," he'd said.

The boys were in awe. On camera, sporting braces and a lisp, Sean called it "the best skate spot I've ever seen."

"And I'm *very* unhappy that we didn't bring my skateboard," he added.

Me, offscreen: "Your life sucks."

Sean, smirking: "It *does*."

One thing about home videos: they can remind you of better times, and your better self.

It's a warm night, late spring, and five boys and their moms and dads are running around our backyard playing dodgeball, shrieking and arguing as the sun begins to set. It's the same crew that had been there the night of Sean's accident almost five years earlier. In the sun-dabbled videos of that night, in every scene we're laughing.

Later, when the skate-themed troubles began, I'd watch those scenes for therapy—both to revisit happier times and to remind myself of our resilience, our ability to recover. In the background bloomed the evidence of what we'd created at Happy Acres: trees we planted, the overgrown garden, the clubhouse on stilts, the paved driveway, the mini skate park.

It had been such a complicated period. Almost losing

Sean. Losing other things. A sense of confidence as a dad, a sense of innocence, a sense of safety. Also losing my mother, who died in 2007 after a terribly long, slow decline. And yet, there we all were on video, my beautiful wife and our friends and a big white dog, all happy and silly and tipsy.

And in the final shot: Leo and Sean fighting over a red ball, rolling in the green grass, like bear cubs.

And then ...

After five happy years at Happy Acres—the longest we'd lived any one place—Mary got a job offer in Seattle, to run the state of Washington's Film Commission. We had already started discussing the need for a family change, believing the boys needed one, too. The trip to Philly had tweaked us all, and we'd realized: the country's been great, but it's time for a city.

We didn't tell the boys about Mary's job right away. Instead, we delivered them to a three-week summer camp, both of them oblivious to the pending life change. Then Mary and I flew to Seattle to find our new home. When we picked the kids up from camp, on the drive home Mary told them: "Okay, so, we've got some pretty big news ..."

"Oh great," said Leo. "You're *pregnant?*"

We handed them each a folder that we'd put together. On the cover were sticker photos of Seattle's Space Needle, the snowcapped mountains, the ferries, Pike Place Market. Inside were pictures of the boys' schools, our new rental house, and prominently, Ballard Bowl skate park and Lower

Woodland Skatepark and Mary sitting in front of a skate shop, decks hanging in a window behind her. The final page was a brochure for an upcoming skate camp. Our move-to-Seattle sales pitch was, blatantly, all about skateboarding.

Leo's reaction: "Holy shit—we get to move to *Seattle?*"

"Leo!" Mary yelled.

"Sorry, it slipped out."

Leo's curse was actually a relief, since we had no idea how they'd react to moving two thousand miles west, swapping their comfy, country lifestyle for a rental in a big city, yet another move (number six) in their wild-goose-bump childhood. While Leo asked excited, eager questions—about Seattle, his school, our house—Sean remained quiet.

"What about the trampoline?" he finally asked, near tears.

ordered a Manhattan, and Mary a martini, and across from us in a cow-patterned booth sat four new friends, our first Friday night date in Seattle.

Both couples had preteen daughters, and the conversation eventually rolled around to the fraught topics of school, sports, academics, activities—the kind of talk that made me uneasy. Mary and I took turns describing our willful sons and their singular passion for skateboarding, and I could tell the other parents were surprised that we'd left them, now ten and twelve, at an indoor skate park for the night. We explained that no, no, it was safe, the kids all looked out for one another, nothing to worry about.

"Better than a babysitter," I said.

Then, just before nine, Leo called, sounding anxious.

"Um . . . Dad? They're closing early. They're asking us to leave."

Shit. The park usually stayed open until eleven. At least I thought so. I left the table to take the call, told Leo to walk with Sean to the sandwich shop a block away.

"Just hang out at Subway until I get there," I said.

Sliding back into the booth, I whispered in Mary's ear, then told our new friends that, ha-ha, silly dad, I had to leave, feeling dumb for ditching our kids without triple-checking when the skate park closed. Then Leo called again.

"Dad, Subway is closing. They said we can't stay here."

Shit.

Within weeks of moving to Seattle, the boys and I had visited every skate park within fifty miles. We drove north to a scruffy park in the San Juan Islands and south to a rain-sopped park in Kurt Cobain's hometown, a dreary lumber town whose welcome sign, quoting Nirvana, read COME AS YOU ARE. Through skating, we discovered our new home, and the boys' cross-country disorientation was offset by greater Seattle's skate scene, which was conveniently experiencing a revival that summer of 2008.

Like many cities, Seattle had had a complicated history with the board. A few skate parks had been demolished in previous years, and skating was still illegal in most public spaces. But a shift was under way. The mayor had recently appointed a Skate Park Task Force to oversee the construction of new parks, including micro "skate dots" to be tucked into city parks, including one near our rental house. The *Seattle Times* editorial board encouraged the city's efforts to "find space for more skate parks," pointing out that skate-boarding was "no longer the obsession of the underground [and] neighborhoods need not fear skaters."

The biggest and busiest new park, Lower Woodland, had opened two months earlier beside some ball fields north of downtown. The boys, now skate park connoisseurs, were impressed by Woodland's deep bowls and sculpted street-skating section, a masterwork of masonry and steel. But they were intimidated by the clots of skinny Seattle teens sucking on cigarettes or swigging Red Bull, a handful of girls ripping tricks that Sean and Leo had yet to master.

Plus, there was the suddenly contentious issue of cranial protection. Back in North Carolina, the skate parks all required signed waivers and helmets and pads. Woodland was a public park, with no oversight and few rules, which meant helmets were optional. Except they weren't for my kids, despite all the "C'mon, *Dad*" pleadings.

Years later, the boys would confess that they often avoided Woodland because they were embarrassed to be in the minority of kids wearing helmets.

Then we found the indoor park called Inner Space, squished beneath a warehouse near a trash transfer station, and it was like they'd entered a holy place. As they took in the low ceilings and fluorescent lights, graffitied basement walls, and shiny-worn concrete floors, the wood-and-steel geometry of hand-built ramps, plywood mani-pads, stair sets, and metal rails, I could tell: in their goggle-eyed reverie, I could've sprouted horns and they wouldn't have noticed.

Cavernous and cacophonous, full of boy howls and cackles, rap music and the clackety clatter of boards, the park was dumpy-cozy, a youth hostel to Woodland's Hyatt. Skaters clustered around the front desk, chugging sodas, mangling Doritos bags, watching skate videos on an ancient TV, lounging on tattered couches. Big industrial fans pushed around warm air, and a garage door opened onto a parking lot where gangly dudes shared smokes.

I couldn't tell who was in charge, but I'd soon learn the place was mostly managed by a serious, skinny guy named Mike. Or sometimes the lanky dreadlocked guy, Chioke, who the boys would learn was either homeless or actually a rich kid acting homeless. Or the cheerful thirty-something named Bean, who often had his hotshot skating toddler son with him. Of huge relief was that, regardless of who ran the place, *everyone* wore a helmet at Inner Space. (Thank you, uptight insurance company.)

I signed waivers and bought the boys ten-visit punch cards and enrolled them in summer day-camp sessions. I felt as if we'd joined a new church.

Inner Space would quickly become their go-to spot, their playground, their after-school babysitter, their Friday night hangout, their first Seattle love. We had traversed the continent but they'd found their ex-pat community, kids who dressed and talked and thought just like them.

When I told others about my kids and their blossoming passion for skating, most would think *Dogtown*—either *Dogtown and Z-Boys*, the documentary narrated by

Sean Penn, or the fictional version, *Lords of Dogtown*. But the style of skating my kids adopted had little to do with empty Southern California swimming pools or the short-shorts, kneesocks, and "sidewalk surfing" of the 1970s Dogtown era.

One reason they loved Inner Space was that it catered to flat-ground, street-skating purists.

The boys once explained it: "vert" skating meant *vertical*, also called park, aerial, or *tranny* (for transitional), which involved high-flying tricks launched from ramps, bowls, and half-pipes modeled after the swimming pools that gave *vert* it's start. "Street" was flat-ground skating, a style built around performing technical tricks onto and off curbs, park benches, stairs, railings, ledges, and other structures— places *not* intended for skating. Vert skating was confined to a half-pipe or skate park, just as team sports were confined to a field or court. But street skating had few physical limits. Vert skating had rules and judges, usually required helmets and pads. Street skating was about *breaking* rules. That was the thrill of the street. As *Thrasher* magazine had declared a quarter century earlier, "The only rules are your own."

Later, in an essay for school, Sean described the appeal: "You don't have a coach or anyone telling you what to do. No signing up, no team you have to join, purely independent, and 100% nondiscriminatory—race, age, gender, size, strength, social skills, background, education, sexual orientation, etc., none of it matters . . . if you skate, you're a skateboarder."

One '90s-era skater positioned skateboarding "at a unique junction of sport and art," one that "reconfigures the public spaces of modern architecture . . . an appropriation of the physical world." I'd soon learn what such sentiments really meant: *trespassing.*

I dropped them off at Inner Space one Friday afternoon and soon got a call from Chioke. Sean and Leo had left with a group of kids and walked to the waterfront beneath Fremont Bridge to skate the steps and ledges surrounding a cluster of corporate office buildings, home to Adobe and Google. A security guard caught them in a parking lot and chased them away, then called Inner Space to complain. Chioke told me by phone that he wasn't comfortable letting preteen boys leave Inner Space on their own.

"Me neither!" I told him, and we agreed that he'd call anytime he or the other managers saw my kids doing something fishy.

Inner Space should've just put me on speed dial.

At the core of all street skating is the ollie. While rolling, a skater stomps the tail and scoops up the nose with the leading edge of their front foot, lifting the board into the air, as if it's glued to their feet. When done right, it looks like a skater is ascending atop a mini hovercraft. (The world record ollie, as of 2017, was just shy of four feet.)

Created by a 1970s vert skater nicknamed Ollie, the trick was pioneered and perfected in the 1980s by skate legend Rodney Mullen, who practiced obsessively in his Florida garage. Compared to the original "ollie air," performed in a bowl or on a ramp, Mullen created the "flat-ground ollie," which would open up the sport to kids who didn't have access to an empty swimming pool, a skate park, or a hill to cruise down. The ollie was revolutionary. It turned driveways and streetscapes into skate parks.

"Nothing in my life up until then had allowed such total creativity," Mullen later told the writer Cole Louison. In describing the liberating freedom of street skating, Louison would use the same words as my kids: "No rules. No coach. No clock . . . No right or wrong way."

Once a skater learned to ollie, they could hop onto a park bench, over a trash bin, maybe one day fling themselves off the top of a set of stairs, even land on a handrail and "grind" all the way down. Armed with an ollie, they entered the realm of outlaw skating, joining the cat-and-mouse game that'd evolved between skaters looking for grindable concrete ledges and authorities trying to prevent what they viewed as vandalism. Look around any public park or plaza and you'll see metal "skate block" devices drilled into ledges that might tempt a skater. You'll also see spots where skaters removed the skate blocks and lubed the ledge with a coat of skate wax.

A gateway trick, the ollie birthed a variety of related feats, such as flicking the board 360 degrees lengthwise in midair, rotisserie-style (a *kickflip*), or whirling it 180 degrees, spin-the-bottle-style (a *pop-shuvit*), or spinning and flipping it at the same time, like those hard-to-comprehend gymnastic twirls (*frontside flip, 360 flip, tre flip*).

But before a skater could dream of tail slides or nose grinds—or half-cabs, nollies, hard flips, heel flips, big flips, or 360s—they had to master the elusive, transformative ollie. Sean and Leo practiced ollies *all* the time, on any paved or concrete surface, driveway, alley, sidewalk, playground, basement, and, maybe inevitably, the street. The first time I caught them doing ollies off a curb near our house, landing just feet from traffic, I shrieked as if I'd caught them carjacking.

"Are you freaking kidding me?" I yelled at Leo. "Have you forgotten already that your brother almost got *killed?*"

And yet? I cheered them on, filmed and photographed them. When Leo asked me to watch him practice in the driveway—"How high, Dad?"—I'd exaggerate, "Six inches!"

Thank god we had a concrete backyard rectangle, and an alley behind that, and a basement with a concrete floor—a rarity in waterlogged Seattle. My office was in a corner of that musty basement, and after a few days of steady rain it'd begin to flood. I'd attack the puddles with an ancient wet-vac so the boys could skate.

I was working down there in my office one day when Sean came down to practice kickflips. Over and over, he'd fall and yell, send his board flying into my desk, creatively cursing in ways that I'd stopped trying to discipline. I turned my music up louder, knowing Sean hated "alternative" music—or, as he put it, Pacific Northwest *hipster* music.

I tapped away at my computer as Sean skated and the rain fell outside and the Shins crooned from my office speakers, until Sean finally landed a kickflip and let out a euphoric "Yes!" I came running and high-fived him.

After sharing our basement moment, I realized: I was getting caught up in it. I had become their enabler.

ince I worked at home, researching my next book and writing freelance magazine articles, I was the after-school dispatcher. Each afternoon, our house became a refueling station for noisy boys who'd stop by for bowls of cereal, fried eggs, panini, some YouTube, some driveway or basement skating. Then they'd flee, in a chattering whorl of boards and backpacks. They were always on the move, rarely inside, and always scheming. When it rained they became impatient and edgy. When it wasn't raining, Mary or I would drive them to their favorite parks, as many boys as we could fit into our minivan, stopping at Dick's Drive-In to load up on sacks of burgers and fries.

I didn't try to become one of them. I didn't take up skating or start dressing like them or, god forbid, listen to their music. I was just *available*. And they didn't seem to mind me hanging around the fringes, videotaping and photographing their tricks, enjoying my role as chronicler—and accomplice.

On weekends, as I had back in North Carolina, I built mani-pads and grind boxes. I got myself a new video camera and posted dorky videos to YouTube, bought the boys their own palm-size digital Flip cameras, and encouraged them to make videos. One Saturday, Leo and I drove to Lowes to get lumber for a new "kicker" ramp. He and I filmed the whole thing—the drive, the construction, Leo's first 180 ollies off the ramp—and turned it into a time-lapse video I called "things skate dads do to keep their kids off drugs."

I was convinced that supporting their passion would one day yield dividends. They'd become filmmakers. Or urban planners. Or contractors. Or, uh . . . architects. Even when the troubles began—the e-mails from teachers, the negotiations with school counselors, security guards, and cops—Mary would joke: "Hey, maybe they'll become *lawyers!*"

Their immersion generated the soundtrack of our daily life, the thwacks and clatters of basement skate sessions, the hip-hop-themed thump of YouTube skate videos. They began speaking a poetic new language, singing of *buttery ledges* and *crispy rails*, of gnarly three-stairs, hips and hubbas, fakies, feebles, footies, varials, wallies, crooks, and crunk.

Driving them to skate parks, I'd listen to their backseat chatter and realize . . . I had no clue. Ever the reporter, I'd sometimes flip on my cell phone's memo recorder to pick up snippets.

One of the boys' friends described a skate spot to my iPhone: "they do rock-to-fakies on the side of that little quarter pipe, that cut-out part of that little bank, and they ollie into that little quarter pipe that goes up to that pillar . . . over by that super gnarly hip." Sean's knowing response: "I'm not gonna lie: rock-to-fakie can be one of the gnarliest tricks ever, especially on super steep tranny, like a wall-ride—if you rock-to-fakie that, that's *sick*." Leo chimed in and described his first rock-to-fakie, but Sean cut him off. "No you didn't, Leo." "Yes I did, Sean." "No way." "Shut up, you weren't there." And so on, until the punches.

When Seattle's rain lingered, the boys binged on skate videos, tapping into the wider world of skating, the skate scenes of Los Angeles, Dallas, Chicago, New York. They'd never been big TV watchers or video gamers, but YouTube became an addiction, their online Skate U. In my hopeful view, it seemed they were learning something about modern America—her cities, geography, people, culture, maybe even some history. When I traveled to San Francisco to research a new book, Sean called with a request. He'd been looking into San Francisco's skate scene and wanted me to visit a famous spot south of downtown known as Third and Army.

"Dad, you *have* to go there for me. *Please?*" Sean insisted. "It's sick."

I found the spot, strolled along the abandoned promenade, beside a toxic-looking creek in a postapocalyptic no-man's-land. I texted pictures to the boys, who no doubt found that more interesting than any of my selfies with astronauts or NASCAR drivers, politicians or authors.

Another symptom of their growing obsession—and our willingness to support it—was the accumulation of skate shoes, an addiction the boys and their friends all shared. Years later, when I'd meet a fellow skate parent, we'd drag one another through the escalating stages and usually shout in unison, "And the shoes! Oh my god, the *shoes!*"

For a birthday or a bribe, we'd buy a pair—"skate shoes," never "sneakers"—and within a week there'd be a hole in the front toe. This was the ollie toe, worn down by repeated scrapings against the board's grip tape: Sean's left toe, and Leo's right, since he (like me) skated in the "goofy footed" stance, right foot forward. A week later, the hole would be gaping, the heels worn thin. After a few weeks of daily use, the shoes would be shreds of canvas and rubber. Convinced

it was a worthwhile investment, we'd give in to their pleading, visit a skate shop, drop another fifty dollars. The shoes
piled up like cordwood, as did inserts and laces, which all
amassed into a musty mudroom mound.

After the shoes came the boards. It's shocking how quickly
a kid can destroy a slab of stamped-together wood and glue.
They began churning through one a month. I'd cringe when
they came home after snapping a board on some trick. A
broken board was like a broken limb—they weren't whole
until we bought a replacement. So, fifty bucks more. Our
house became a Museum of Broken Boards, a menagerie of
battered retirees and broken half shards, sentimental favorites saved on shelves, hung by wire on a wall.

When they were feeling low, or needy, or out of sync with
the world? When the pressures of being the new kid in school
bore down on them? Skate shoes or a fresh board made life
right again. Mary and I, antimaterialistic in most other
ways, willingly helped them become aficionados of footwear
from Vans, Adidas, DC, Etnies, Nike. We became patrons
of shops like Goods, 35th North, and Zumiez, and occasionally splurged on boards from Girl, Chocolate, Manik, or
Enjoi. Our skate-themed house also collected trucks, nuts,
wheels, bolts, bearings, skate wrenches, bars of wax, coils
of grip tape, tangles of shoelaces, stacks of skate magazines,
and the spread of posters across bedroom walls.

I rarely subjected the boys to that fatherly "when I was
your age" guilt trope, though I'd sometimes torment myself
with it. *When I was their age* . . . I played baseball, football,
and guitar; I read books and newspapers; I had an early-

morning paper route. Still, I was never as passionate about those things as the boys were about skating. They'd found something to call their own. It gave them an identity. And they were doing it *together*—unlike me and my brother, who started to drift apart as we neared high school.

Mary and I decided that skating made them happy, and that *mattered*. It kept them outdoors, active, and fit. It earned them friends, tied them to a community. It kept two brothers close. "They *need* this, right!? It's who they are now," Mary once said, after picking them up from some grungy South Seattle skate park. "What choice do we really have here?"

And yet . . . I wondered whether we'd been ignoring a few warning signs.

PART 2
KICKFLIPPING OUT

5

S ean's math teacher e-mailed us to let us know she'd caught him reading a skateboarding magazine in class, hiding it behind his workbook. She also sometimes caught him skating a fingerboard across his desk or textbook. It might've been funny if he hadn't been struggling in her class. He doodled. He daydreamed. And he defied.

On one assignment Sean wrote "I DON'T WANT TO" surrounded by frowny faces. On a test he answered each question with the word *scribbles*. A few days later, his math teacher called again, having caught him drawing graffiti on a desk—a big bubble-shaped *F* that Sean insisted was going to be *flow*, not the other four-letter *F* word.

Suddenly, when it came to anything unrelated to skating, my sixth grader was disinterested at best, disdainful at worst. Or just sad. In one notebook Sean wrote "I hate this school" *dozens* of times. I found a computer printout with

"I HATE MY LIFE" filling the whole page. Our efforts to comfort or coach him were often rebuffed. Both boys increasingly resisted parental input. Why not join the art club? *Nah.* Audition for the school play? *Nah.* Try ultimate Frisbee? Tennis? Track? *No. No. No.*

When we enrolled them in an after-school kids' club, a place for board games and kickball and homework, they whined and moaned as if we'd signed them up for a daily dental exam. "Why can't I just go skating with my friends?" Sean wanted to know. The answer—"because you're only *twelve*"—made no sense. They'd "accidentally" miss the van to the club and regularly bent or broke all the rules. Sean, Leo, and two friends once wandered away from a field trip, telling the counselors that I was picking them up nearby. On the van ride back to the club, a counselor saw the four boys sticking their heads into a different kind of club, called Showgirls. A half-clad hostess shooed them off.

Not until the club counselors let them bring their skateboards did the boys willingly attend, though they bitched about having to wear helmets.

I felt an acceleration into a new phase of boyhood. They were still my little guys, still huggy and affectionate, unashamed to tell their parents and each other "I love you."

But at ten and twelve, the teen years beckoned, and a mini-me voice in my head taunted, "Hey man, you know what's coming, don't you?"

I'm not sure why I was caught so flat-footed. From personal experience I knew, or should have known, that skating was about more than *skating*, just as surfing was about more than catching waves. Riding boards—skate or surf or snow—had long been a sport-slash-mindset associated with flipping convention the bird, the way other fuck-you messages, from tattoos to fast cars to rock and roll to teen sex, told parents, *It's my life.* But I also knew—again, personal experience—that a reasonable pursuit of freedom and independence (skating's unspoken core tenets) could burn some creative self-reliance into kids who might be destined to become actors, filmmakers, artists, musicians. Or even writers.

So. As my boys adopted the whole ethos, the fashion and the music, the art and the language, I did what an ex-skater turned skate dad was expected to do. I tolerated. I abided.

And braced myself for some messy karma.

My friend Don and I are arcing down a gleaming ribbon of black, virgin asphalt, smooth and shimmery as a panther's back, not yet spoiled by car tires.

We get to the bottom, walk up, skate it again, over and over, weaving through rocks and lumber we've set as our obstacle course. Construction workers are gone for the day, leaving the half-built Cardinal Hills housing development all to us, especially this fresh-paved slope, this perfect wave. We're fast, we're thirteen, and we're free.

Don rides a thin, flexy blue fiberglass board, and I'm on a thick hard-plastic board with a kick tail, banana yellow. Don is the better skater, just as he's become the better skier and water-skier. In all of our board riding, with the ski club and the waterskiing team, Don has always been bolder. I once watched him ride his skateboard off a plywood ramp, up and over a few neighborhood kids lined up like logs. Cruising downhill, he's loose and in control, showing none of the trepidation that constricts me. On foot, Don is gawky, a bit pudgy; on a skateboard, on snow skis and water skis, he's all confident grace and sashaying fluidity.

Today, the sun droops and we make one last descent, slaloming our entwined S's down this beautiful black asphalt. We stop at the bottom, where Don's board suddenly shoots out from beneath his feet, nose-first into a concrete curb. I can still picture the rest, in a hazy slow-motion: Don looks surprised as he tilts backward, parallel to the ground, his arms leaning back to break his fall, one of them getting folded behind his back, then the sickeningly loud *snap* as Don breaks his arm with his own ass.

He shouts and curses, but it doesn't last. He stands and we both gawk at his crooked forearm like it's some artifact, a dead snake or cat.

"Guess I'll see you tomorrow," Don says, grabbing his board, cradling his arm, and I feel bad letting him walk home alone, but I'm afraid I'll get in trouble.

We were always doing stupid shit, me and Don. A combustible duo. Unchecked, dumb-ass, preteen boys.

Stupid shit? It's what we lived for.

I grew up in New Jersey, an hour northwest of New York City, in a pretty village of Tudor homes circling a lake dotted by beaches. My dad, an electrical engineer, joined the eastward flood of commuters each morning. My mom, a nurse, had stopped working when my sister, Maura, was born, two years before me, with Down syndrome.

My parents had soundly rejected doctors' advice to put Maura in a home, and my mom devoted herself to giving my sister as normal a childhood as possible. My mom lobbied for Maura's inclusion in regular classrooms long before the "mainstreaming" of disabled students became a movement. She taught Maura to read and enrolled her in sports. Despite a bum knee that would confine her to a wheelchair, Maura proudly competed in the Special Olympics, events like the Frisbee fling and softball toss (she was a lefty, like Sean), collecting a shoe box full of ribbons and medals. In a newspaper story I wrote about the 1995 Special Olympics, I quoted then-President Clinton who, at the opening ceremonies, told the assembled athletes: "The world can learn a great lesson from all of you standing here tonight. Everybody counts and everybody can do something very important and very good."

It was a lesson I'd learned the hard way. Some days we'd be pushing Maura through the mall in her wheelchair, and some kids or even grown-ups would stare, point, or laugh. I'd stare or point back, or sometimes confront them, Jersey style: "Whatta you looking at? Got a *problem?*" But Maura never got ruffled. She would just smile at them.

Maura. The beautiful glow at the center of our family. My happy big sister with the pure mind of a child, who loved listening to her albums, which numbered in the hundreds, who loved strumming her guitar and plunking at her electric piano, who loved watching sitcoms and old movies from a massive VHS collection. She loved Elvis and the Osmonds, *The Brady Bunch* and *The Sound of Music*. She loved her parents, her dog and cat, her brothers, her occasional boyfriends. When you were with Maura, she'd look at you like you were all that mattered. She loved like no one I'd ever met, or ever would. Her love gave me strength, a superpower. Maura's love fortified me. It also, unintentionally, liberated me.

Not that my parents didn't also "raise" me and my younger brother, Jeff. But from an early age we were told: You guys can take care of yourselves. Maura can't. Just be home for dinner.

Which gave Jeff and me all the freedom little boys crave, plus some. We created our own *Where the Wild Things Are* lifestyle, a wild suburban rumpus. In our cozy 1970s lake community, most neighbor kids were allowed to roam the woods and beaches as much as we were, it's just that some of us took advantage of that freedom.

That's how Jeff and I met Don and his brother, Steve. They lived half a mile away, but we found each other. We were the ones who could roam a little farther, stay out a little later. For a while, our primary playground was the sprawling construction of the development that slowly turned the woods behind our neighborhood into an amusement park for boys: bulldozers and backhoes, sewer pipes and lumber, half-built homes and fresh-paved streets.

In between skate sessions, Don and I broke into those homes, pretended to drive the backhoes, crabbed deep into concrete drainage pipes. We once crawled a quarter mile through dank blackness to find a sewer exit blocked, and had to turn around and shimmy back. Our hangout was a clump of tree stumps that'd formed a small cave, which we dubbed the Playboy Palace. In the "PBP" we stowed stolen firecrackers, cigarettes, empty beer cans, decorated it with 1960s *Playboy* centerfolds pinched from my attic.

We talked about girls we loved, guys we hated. We made fart and dick jokes. We smoked cigarettes and planned our next naughty adventures.

Unlike Don or my brother, I'd played lots of sports throughout childhood, most of them (like my academics) at roughly a C+ level. When I discovered my boards, I excelled.

First came skis: a gift from an aunt and uncle, blue planks on which I'd ski in our backyard, ten slushy feet at a time. Next came waterskiing. By six I could slalom, and by eight I could jump. Then another aunt and uncle gave Jeff and me skateboards for Christmas, bullet-shaped slabs of wood atop clay wheels that, skated side by side, sounded like dueling cement mixers. Though I kept playing baseball and football, I found something exciting and new on my skateboards, skis, and water skis. Having a handicapped sister often felt like nursing a secret, like I knew something my peers didn't. In a similar way, veering from ball sports to board sports made me feel like I'd found a secret path.

Weeks after starting second grade in a new school, I tripped over my shoelaces, conked my head, and poked a hole in my palm with a pencil. I sat there gushing blood until a classmate called out, "Miss Cahill, the new boy is bleeding."

My mom came to get me, the doctor patched me up, and the next day my dad let me stay home—and took me waterskiing. I remember my dad's friends drinking cans of beer and being impressed by a seven-year-old who could slalom with a sutured hand in a plastic bag. I felt unique, weird, special.

In time, Don became my prime board-riding partner. He and I skied at our puny ski area with the Sparta Ski Club. In summer we joined the Ski Hawks waterskiing team, competing in slalom events, performing pyramids with girls on our tanned shoulders, carving tricks and launching jumps at the annual Fourth of July shows on the lake, including the show where I sliced open a fallen teammate's forehead. On our skateboards, we reveled in the freedom of not needing a ski lift or a boat to tow us. The ollie hadn't been invented and there were no nearby skate parks, but all we needed was a slope of pavement, down which we'd slalom at dusk.

My brother found similar freedom on his bicycle. Jeff became that neighborhood kid who craved speed and air—and risk. He twice almost got hit by cars, once riding his Big Wheel down our lawn and into the street, and once sledding into the street. He built ramps to jump his bike over garbage cans and, like Don, over our trusting friends. I remember one dad screaming as Jeff lined up for an Evel Knievel–style jump over a row of eight kids. It hadn't occurred to us that number eight might get a tire in the face.

As kids, my brother and our friends, we did dicey, boyish things. We sought them out with a vengeance. And we were just getting started.

And now, with my kids on a path that reminded me of

me, and of Jeff, and of Don, I felt a confusing mix of pride, nostalgia ... and dread.

When their interest in skating began, my boys had come at it from slightly different angles. Leo was initially more interested in the sport, while Sean was fascinated by the culture. Leo was drawn to the social scene, the collegiality of the skate park, while Sean preferred the fringes, the harder edge of the trespassing street-skating scene. Leo was the happy-go-lucky risk taker, while Sean was the diva, throwing passionate tantrums when he failed to land a trick, sometimes snapping his own board in anger.

Sean had always been more complicated. Aunts and uncles would ask, "How do you get *through* to Sean?" Teachers now wondered the same. He was thoughtful, curious, and kind, but the world confused him and, increasingly, bugged him. He constantly fought for more freedom and less responsibility than school life and home life allowed. "Don't you think there's something wrong with the world we live in?" he had asked years earlier—at age *eight*. "Shouldn't everyone be able to do what they want to do?"

It's a question that now hovered devilishly around Sean's head. In most dealings with an adult—teacher, counselor, parent—his knee-jerk response to a request was, *Why should I?* Like a mash-up of Peter Pan and Bartleby the Scrivener, Sean's boyhood take on life's expectations was becoming: "I would prefer not to."

He "lost" worksheets and notebooks, forgot pens and textbooks. The word *no* became a Tourette's-like tick. He could get As on tests, but sometimes didn't see the point. A few teachers saw something inside and tried to coax it out. Others, perplexed by his resistance, frustrated by their inability to connect, would shrug and move on, the start of a trend that I worried would pit Sean against his future, would brand him as unteachable.

One night Mary dropped the boys at Inner Space for '80s night, sponsored by a local skate company, Manik, that would give free T-shirts to the best 1980s outfits. The boys did their best Beastie Boys impressions—baggy white tees, jeans pulled low, neck chains—happily costumed in a way that reminded me of the not-so-distant days of Power Ranger suits and plastic sword fights. Back home, Mary and I ate dinner, drank some wine, and talked about the strange new phase we seemed to have entered.

"Maybe I just need to know more about what it means to be a boy," Mary said that night. "I feel like there's a word I want to make up for what they're going through—like, I dunno . . . *dysperia*."

Later that week, Sean had a couple math problems to do for homework and could've banged it out in five minutes. Instead, he sat at the kitchen table stewing, doodling, fingerboarding, then laying his head on the notebook, pissed at the whole concept. When he refused to set the table for dinner, I took away the fingerboard, and he accused me of ruining his life. "Why do you hate me? You should just kill me!" he screamed. Then, minutes later: "I just want a hug!" *Dysperia?*

At times it was painful to watch. Also painful were his

rejections of our attempts to help. Mary and I veered daily from compassion to frustration to anger to punishment and back. At its core: Sean simply didn't like being told what to do. By anyone. He also preferred the drama of defiance to the quiet of compliance. Skateboarding totally stoked this attitude.

And, because brothers stick together, Leo began to adopt a similar contempt for obedience. Grumbling once about a teacher: "He's the dullest knife in the drawer. He's a freakin' spoon. A *plastic* spoon." Baby-faced Leo was developing a temper, too, and a potty mouth, a jarring thing to witness in a kid who looked years younger than his age, who'd believed in Santa Claus (or at least wanted to) until age ten. I once overheard him arguing with a wrong-number dialer . . .

"I'm an eleven-year-old kid, there's no way I'm your *fucking* landlord."

Mary and I developed a new routine, running or walking through various Seattle neighborhoods, exploring parks, paths, and alleys, searching for a house to someday buy. Mary usually outpaced me. She'd stop and do stretches, waiting for me to catch up. With her untamed hair, yoga pants, and running shoes, still looking like the twenty-nine-year-old I first met, I'd watch her pinch rosemary sprigs or lavender buds and rub the fragrant herbs into her hands. She adored the perfumed lushness of the Pacific Northwest, the exploding spring colors, incapable of bypassing a rosebush without sampling.

She'd give me shit for not sharing her enthusiasm: "Why do you hate flowers?"

During our walks we'd talk about the boys, school, and skating. Other nights we'd each get lost in our thoughts, and she'd start pulling farther away.

"Hey," I'd yell, trying to keep up. "Want to walk together like a couple?"

Watching her walk ahead sometimes reminded me of our Costa Rican honeymoon and the day we hiked away from our rustic resort. We swam naked in a cove and both sprinted back out at the same time, tweaked by a sense that sharks were lurking. We stopped at a farmer's hut, begging for *agua*, which we forgot to bring, then chugged his offering of warm beer. Returning to camp we came across a German family photographing a tree pulsing with a flock of parrots. After a respectful few minutes, Mary said, "Sorry, coming through," and continued along the path as scores of parrots fluttered and fled, an exploding rainbow, as the camera-toting Germans cursed.

Tonight, she walked with that same determined strut, but suddenly stopped beneath the canopy of a white-bloomed cherry tree . . .

"Do you think the skating is a mistake?" she asked. "I mean, maybe there's a reason other parents keep their kids away from skate parks."

She tossed a handful of cherry blossoms in the air, turned, and kept walking, leaving me in her dust.

6

Though I sometimes worried that skating was an accelerant for Sean's preteen yips, there was no denying he found peace on his board, a place that made sense, where he was in full control, with no parents or teachers setting expectations or conveying their disappointment. And Leo? When he dropped into a deep bowl or popped a perfect kickflip or costarred in a YouTube video that he shot and edited himself? He wasn't the shortest kid, his size didn't matter, and the board and the park defined him in ways that nothing else could.

Skating made them happier than any activity, so the boards came along wherever we went as a family, tucked awkwardly beneath our table at a restaurant, crammed into the car trunk, squeezed into overhead train or airplane bins. Like the stuffed animals they'd only recently semiretired—Poly the polar bear for Leo; Twiggy the yellow bunny for

Sean—the boards could never be left behind. "Skate trip" and "skate vacation" entered our vocabulary.

One weekend I took the boys north to Vancouver on Amtrak. We dumped our bags at a cheap hotel and hit the streets. I videotaped them skating through meth-head sections of the city's Chinatown. At a gritty skate park splayed beneath highway overpasses and train tracks, I filmed Leo, on his first try, landing a frighteningly huge full-speed ollie off a five-foot ledge—a ledge taller than he was. Had he missed, he and his helmet-less skull would've sampled Canada's touted health care.

After nailing his flying ollie, Leo coolly rolled past me, flashing #1 fingers—"First try, *Dad!*"—then fist-bumped his brother. Later, as I added a soundtrack and posted the video to YouTube, feeling proud of our skate trip adventures, our quirky father-son togetherness, I realized, as Mary once put it: What choice did we really have here? I kept buying shoes and boards, filming and photographing them, sanctioning this sport that kept us together, even if something about the skate-vs.-school mismatch nagged at me.

By now, Sean and Leo had created their own personal fight club. It didn't take much—"Dude, don't look at me like that"—before they were entangled on the floor like two octopi. Boy fighting was a constant in our life. As in every. Single. Day. From their twos to their teens, the same screams and crying, the same weapons (plastic swords, boxing gloves, kitchen implements, fists), and often the same script . . .

Get off of me dawg, Jesus . . . I didn't mean to punch you in the mouth I meant to punch you in the neck . . . What the hell's wrong with you bro—goddam!

You started it . . . It's not my fault . . . Get off me, bro . . . I'll beat your ass . . . Ow, that hurts . . . Cry about it . . . I can't breathe . . . Ow, OW! Mom, Dad!

Some fights took on a new edge. One night we watched a *Glee* episode that tackled the topic of bullying. I told the boys how kids had picked on my sister, called her retard or 'tardo, how I'd always despised bullies. It seemed like a good chat, but soon Sean was chasing Leo around the house, squirting him with a turkey baster, tormenting him until Leo cried.

I finally intervened and smacked Sean atop his head. Mary and I rarely resorted to corporal punishment. I could've counted on one hand the number of times I'd actually spanked them. So a swat on the head got Sean's attention. Furious, he grabbed his skateboard and ran from the house. I found my boy an hour later, half a mile from home, outside a dumpy doughnut shop. He'd skated there and was sitting atop his board in the rain. I hugged him, he got in the car, and we drove home in silence.

I remembered drives like that with my parents, nothing to say, the car filled with a cloud of teenage rage. As a dad, I hated such shitty moments. I hated being the enforcer.

Leo, meanwhile, seemed torn. He wanted to support his angsty brother, but he also wanted family peace. He was learning to play the middle. The peacemaker.

For his eleventh birthday, we took Leo and friends to a paintball place, where I accidentally shot him in the neck (he was *furious*) and Mary shot me (accidentally?) in the crotch. That night, we let Leo stay out late, and when he got home I spied a text on his cell phone: "was that ur 1st kiss?" I interrogated Sean, who told me Leo had played truth or dare with two neighbor girls. A week later, more cell phone spying revealed that Leo had been texting both girls, one of whom got mad when she spotted him with the other.

His reply: "I'm with both of you."

Leo was like that at home, too: his brother's defender when Sean needed him; conciliator when Mary and I needed him. Leo adapted to whoever needed him more. He volunteered to set the table, fill water glasses, wash dishes, take out the trash. He sought out household jobs but also lobbied like a union rep for more pay. He'd later call it "chores for cheddar." One night, as Sean flopped in homework-aversion agony on the couch, Leo asked me and Mary, "How about I make you guys a martini?"

He'd seen us mix plenty over the years—more so in recent months. Manhattans, too. He surely knew they had magical, family-calming qualities. Mary and I exchanged looks: *Is this wrong?* I handed Leo *Hemingway & Bailey's Bartending Guide* and told him, "Vodka, not gin. And not too much vermouth." Leo's martinis became a semiregular predinner event. I videotaped him one night, pouring and shaking like a tiny Tom Cruise in *Cocktail*, and edited together a Vimeo clip I called "Leo the Bartender."

But . . . was the intensity in our household getting to him?

Were Sean's battles against homework, chores, and parenting, and my increasingly shrill and shouted responses, doing some damage?

One night Leo and I talked about the possibility of a new middle school for Sean, and I shared my concerns about them drifting apart the way my brother and I did when we'd ended up at different high schools. "That'd *never* happen with me and Sean," Leo assured me. "It's just . . . I just want him to come home happy. I want *us* to be happy."

I hadn't quite realized that we'd become *un*-happy. Another night, after mixing martinis—olives for me, a twist for Mary—then helping prep and clean up dinner, with Sean complaining about an assignment in an overly dramatic British accent ("It's too *haaaahd*"), Leo pulled Mary aside and asked if they could have "a private talk."

Mary suggested a walk. By now she'd become a world-class neighborhood walker. As they strolled down the street and across the playground at Leo's school, Mary waited until Leo was ready. "I feel like a ghost in my own house," he said, then talked for thirty straight minutes about school, friends, teachers, girls, skating . . . and death.

"I just don't understand what *happens*," he said.

Leo also, for some reason, told Mary he was worried about divorce.

"Are you and Fudge-luff okay?" he asked, using the nickname the boys had given me.

The name came from Leo's toddler-era mispronunciation of father, which had sounded like *fah-zhah*. It evolved over time into a term of endearment that sounded like Persian cheese, *fuszhe-luv*, then Fudge-luff or Fudge Love or Fudgie. Mary became Mumzhluv, Mumslo, Mums Loaf, Mumzie, or Mum.

"Mumslo?" Leo asked. "Are *we* going to be okay?"

When two of Sean's classmates got expelled for smoking pot in the bathroom—and one of the pot smoker's friends was arrested for bringing a handgun to school—that's when we decided it was time for a new school. We switched Sean from his public school teeming with a thousand students to a private school with sixty kids and a dozen teachers, crammed beneath a bank in the International District.

Personally, I worried that the choice of schools might not matter, that all teachers were overworked, underpaid, and generally ill-equipped to get through to kids who viewed teachers through the same lens they viewed cops. But Sean was game for a change, and his application questionnaire spoke to his need for a new scene:

When are you happiest? "I am happiest when skateboarding."
When are you most proud? "I'm most proud of being myself."
What do you like to do with your free time? "Skateboard. Period."
Use five adjectives to describe yourself. "Hyper, Active, Anxious, Clueless, Bored."

Mary and I hoped a small private school would nurture Sean, help him feel better about himself, and as Mary wrote in our portion of the application, "build confidence and trust, and reengage him with a community so he can start learning and enjoy school . . . and hopefully help him reconnect to that core person inside."

As I watched my wife (an A student in her day) spend an hour completing the parent section of the application, I realized: she is as worried as I am . . .

"At his core, Sean is a thoughtful, intelligent, creative, curious, and loving person," Mary wrote. "Someone who knows what's right and wrong and wants to do the right thing; someone who has ambitions to excel at things (like skateboarding) and create things (like videos) and explore the world around him."

Sean's new school let him bring his board, let him skate in the parking lot at lunch, even offered to let him build his own lesson plan around skateboarding. He could study its history and culture, the marketing and economics of today's skate scene. We briefly felt like we'd won some academic lotto for our school-wary son.

But Sean? He still preferred not to. Bit by bit he rebelled against the most lenient academic institution in Seattle.

"I'm seeing another side of Sean," the earnest principal told Mary, after initially assuring us that he'd "dealt with lots of kids like Sean" and "he'll be fine here."

The end came quickly. Sean developed a rivalry with a student who was bullying another kid. One day, in defense of the victim, Sean took justice into his own hands and hid the bully's iPhone and sneakers. Teachers called a school-wide meeting to get to the bottom of things. Sean initially pretended that he knew nothing about the missing iPhone. But the evidence crowded in on him. He grew angry that *he* was getting in trouble, not the bully. And then he lost it, declaring the whole "community concept" bogus.

"This isn't real life," he told the gathering of students and teachers, then turned to the principal: "Your methods are *flawed!*"

In our subsequent—and final—meeting, the principal told me he'd never had a student stand up to him like that. "I'm not sure what to make of Sean," he said, with a mix of what I read as admiration and disappointment and, I think, fear. "I've never met anyone quite like him . . ." He suggested we consider another school for seventh grade.

In a follow-up e-mail, one of Sean's teachers tried to ease the pain of our failed private school experiment: "I want to be sure you both know that I really came to love and appreciate Sean in the short time we had together. On Friday he came to say good-bye . . . and we had a connection in that moment that was piercingly tender and tearful. Thank you for the time with your beautiful son, and thank you for taking a stand for him as his parents, making the tough calls, and doing courageous work."

Courageous? That's not how it felt. I had hoped that a small private school might do some heavy lifting for me, make my kid care about learning. Of course, middle school can be a downer for any kid, but in Sean's case we worried that the transition from hippie-hillbilly Asheville to a gritty big city was more jarring than we realized.

One night, Sean pulled Mary aside for a talk and told her, "It's all Daddy's fault, you know."

"What's Daddy's fault?" she asked.

"*Everything.*"

I was glad one of us, with her walk-and-talk therapy sessions, was getting through. But I also worried Sean was right. He and Leo had grown from toddlers into boys in a lush and magical place called Happy Acres. Then we changed the rules, yanked them from their comfort zone, across the country, and forced them to grow into teens in grunge city.

Reaching the end of our first Seattle school year, a year after our move west, felt like wobbling across the finish line with a flat tire and no gas. We decided to pack the boards and head back east for a weeklong stay with Mary's parents. We tooled around Asheville, visiting the boys' friends and mine, day-tripping past the playgrounds and landmarks of their childhood, including the house where we'd almost lost Sean. As we pulled up to the same spot where he got nailed by that silver Corolla, the boys looked up at the house—"our swing is still there!"—while I looked left, at the grassy spot where Sean says he died and saw God.

At downtown's Food Lion Skatepark, the boys skated with a former grade school pal, and I watched the three of them, all pale and bony arms, skinny-fuzzy legs, in their tank tops and required helmets, gliding into the same bowl where Leo had first learned to drop in, the place where their passion for skating was ignited.

That afternoon we drove out to Happy Acres. The warm air and bouncy light brought it all back, the memories of our off-the-grid place (which we still owned and rented to tenants), this strange homestead in the misty mountains where my little men had lived *half* their lives. No wonder city life in Seattle had fucked us all up some.

On the way back down the hill, we passed the turnoff where I'd taken the call from my dad just two years earlier.

"Neal?" his shaky voice had said that day, and I'd known in an instant . . . my mother was gone.

Her death began twenty years earlier.

I was living with two friends in Philadelphia, working as a stringer at the *Inquirer*, paid by the story, no benefits, but a dream job. I sat beside the *Inquirer*'s mob reporter, worked with reporters and editors who had won Pulitzers, who had written books. This was the start of my writing career. I bought a car, got a credit card, wore a tie. I covered murder trials and elections. I saw my first dead body, scored my first A-1 story. I was twenty-three. My writing life—my *life* life—was about to begin.

Early one morning the phone rang, and my roommate banged on my door.

"Neal, wake up, it's your dad!"

In a quavering voice—the same one I'd recognize twenty years later—my dad said that he'd come home to find my mom crumpled and bleeding on the basement floor. She'd fallen down the stairs and hit her head. They'd airlifted her from our local hospital to a head trauma unit in Allentown. She was in a coma. She needed surgery. He told me to hurry.

My mom was still in a coma ten days later when her mother, my eighty-year-old Irish grandma, Della, fell down the steps of her apartment in Perth Amboy, New Jersey. My uncle found her, and we eulogized and buried her while my mom continued her deep sleep in Allentown.

On one of my trips to visit my mom, I bought a $600 word processor at the Allentown mall, one of my first big credit card purchases. At the hospital, I started writing a short story about a newspaper reporter whose brain-injured mother awakes from a coma and doesn't recognize him. "Where's my son? The boy . . . Where's what's his name?"

After a transfer to a rehab center in New Jersey, followed by months of physical and occupational therapy, my mother went on to make a slow but impressive recovery. I'd always credit Maura for helping her pull through, for holding her hand during our hospital visits and transmitting some sort of telepathic daughter-mother SOS. Something deep inside my mother's wounded head must have gotten the message "Maura needs you. Wake up!" She did, three weeks after her fall, and she healed—far beyond doctors' expectations—but still, there were gaps . . . She was still our mom, still Pat, but an 80 percent version. She stopped shy of a full recovery.

Seven years after my mother's accident, I was living in New York with Mary when I received another early-morning phone call, this time from my brother.

My sister had passed out. Jeff and my mom were driving her to the hospital. I frantically dug my old BMW out of the snow on Riverside Drive, a few blocks from the cathedral where Mary and I had married a year earlier. During an excruciating wait for the windows to defrost, I flashed back to our wedding. My lone regret about that otherwise beautiful April day was that I never danced with my sister. My mom later told me that Maura had been waiting for me to ask her to dance, a memory that tormented me.

I raced an hour west on I-80. At the hospital, my dad arrived a few minutes after I did, and we awkwardly embraced, probably our first hug since I was a toddler. Standing outside the ER, the doctor told us Maura had had a massive stroke.

"She won't survive this," he flatly declared.

They got her settled in a room and we all sat watching the monitors, stroking her hands, her hair, her face. I pressed my cheek against hers and whispered in her ear, telling her how much she meant to me, how she inspired me, empowered me. From my sister I learned what it meant to be compassionate, tolerant. I could tap into that superpower when I needed a jolt of strength. Without her, I'd be . . . *normal?*

I begged Maura to stay alive a little longer, at least until Mary could get there to say good-bye. And Maura did it, she waited. Hours later, Mary arrived from the TV commercial she'd been shooting, nervous and confused, too new to my weird family. She hugged Maura and said good-bye and I loved her for that. Within twenty minutes Maura's heart slowed further, as did the machine blips, slower and slower until she was gone.

Sean was born a year later, and relatives came to our new house in New Jersey to check out this kid with the spiky hair and goofy grin, and I'd hold him in my arms and think how much Maura would've loved being an aunt. And my mom? Oh, she would have been such a cool grandma. But she never really got the chance.

She and my dad moved to Florida after Maura died, and she began acting strange, wandering from home, arguing with neighbors, showing signs of dementia that doctors attributed to her head injury. She slid backward, from 80 percent, to 70, and on down. Mary and I moved once more, from New Jersey to Maryland, where Leo was born. My mom came to visit, and I'd find her in the bathroom talking to herself in the mirror, talking to Maura. I was afraid to let her hold her new grandson and would make her sit down first, then carefully hand her bubbly baby Leo.

Back in Florida, walking down the street, my mother fell and hit her head. Another coma. She was hospitalized for weeks, the start of a terrible decline that lasted a decade, the last half of those years in a nursing home. What should have been golden days of sunshiny retirement for my parents instead became a series of hospitalizations, injuries, illnesses, meds. My dad kept working to cover the bills, and I think to keep himself sane. My boys never got to know their grandmother, only the childlike shell she became.

When my mother died and my dad had called me that day in North Carolina, I'd pulled over and parked beside a cornfield and cried, choking sobs that took nearly an hour to subside. Then I went for an hours-long hike in the rain.

At her funeral, in the church where I'd once been an altar boy, with her coffin parked in the same spot Maura's had stood a dozen years earlier, I walked to the pulpit and spoke about "vivacious, life-loving Pat . . . a strong, independent woman . . . funny, witty, sarcastic, irreverent." I talked about the Pat I knew before her accidents, the one who gabbed with strangers, who devoured fat romance novels, who loved to cook, who loved thrift stores, tea, chablis, who devoted herself to Maura and others like Maura.

More than anything I wanted Sean and Leo to hear who their grandmother had been. I called her "a quiet hero." Behind me sat Father McHugh, who'd also helped us bury Maura, the good man who'd kicked me out of high school—something I joked about in my eulogy—who'd been a constant in my family's life for decades.

I choked up only once, when I mentioned my dad, whose quiet strength and devotion to Pat over the years had humbled me.

Pat was buried beside Maura, beneath a tombstone preengraved with her name, and my dad's name.

After the funeral, I gave Mary and the boys a tour of my hometown. It was the Fourth of July weekend, and as we walked through the village and along the boardwalk we caught the tail end of the annual waterskiing show, the same show where Don and I had performed. We later explored town, and the flashbacks went *pop, pop, pop.* Here was the stationery shop where Don and I shoplifted pricey pens. There was the playground where I chugged my first beer, choked on cigarettes. Here was the beach where I'd kissed my first girl. There was the trail where I fell down laughing, tripping on mushrooms with Dennis and Dave. And here was the street where I cruised atop my first skateboard.

Now, two years after losing Pat, a year into our new life in Seattle, with my kids entering their middle school years, I desperately wanted to call her, beg her to clue me in to the mysteries of raising of two boys. Pat used to send me letters at college, and one day I found a few buried at the bottom of a lockbox, including the one where she gave me shit for some test I'd apparently decided to skip. "I guess I'm upset that you would just give up without giving it your best shot," she wrote.

"But this is your life, Neal T," she added, in her very Pat-like blend of motivation plus Irish-Catholic guilt. "Do what you think is best. And drive safe."

I also found in the lockbox a worn-out newspaper clipping she'd sent me, a hokey poem called "The Man in the Glass." I remembered that back in college I thought it was silly, but for some reason I'd saved it all those years. As I held the frayed clipping in my hand, it seemed like she was reaching out to me, reminding me of something . . .

> It isn't your father or mother or wife
> Whose judgment upon you must pass
> The fellow whose verdict counts most in your life
> Is the one staring back from the glass

7

To a skater, a sunny day beckoned like fresh powder to a skier, like an undulating swell to a surfer.

At the end of sun-teased school days, the boys would crash into the mudroom, fling backpacks, snatch boards, yell "Bye, Dad!" and be smoke before I could ascend from the basement. On weekends, they'd start scheming by noon, dialing and texting, making plans that'd keep them on the streets until dusk and beyond, squeezing the last drop from each day.

When the inevitable Seattle rains came, the boys learned to adapt, finding shelter beneath Seattle's streets. Underground they went, into subterranean stairwells, loading docks, parking garages, beneath department stores, shopping malls, schools, and corporate office parks. Internet and YouTube tips unlocked for them the secrets of skating in the rain.

One favorite spot was below a QFC grocery store. Level 1 was too risky, busy with grocers and the occasional store manager. But Level 2? Only residents of the condos stacked above QFC had access. The boys would hover near the residents-only entrance, feigning nonchalance. When a condo owner swiped their card, they'd wait for the car to pass through, then hop on their boards and skate down the ramp past the closing gate. They called this spot T-Fac, for Training Facility, their secret workshop for new tricks. Eventually QFC hired a security guard—"I think that was because of us," Sean later told me—but even then, on good days they'd get in a few hours of skating before security came "beefin'."

The spot beneath the Adobe and Google offices demanded a similar strategy. Elevators to the garage required a pass card, so the boys would sneak through the front doors and wait near the elevators, hoping for a nonthreatening employee to swipe their card and hit a parking-level button. The trick, as Sean later explained, was to trust those unlikely to snitch, ideally a bearded young engineer, all flannel and jeans—former skater?—like the guy Sean once described who shrugged, punched "P1," and said, "No skin off my balls."

Cops, security guards, and store managers were always a-prowl. In fact, conflicts with security guards may have been among the more meaningful adult relationships they had at that age. After getting kicked out of the same places over and over, they got to know a few by name. Some were hard-ass rent-a-cops, but others were occasionally lenient, even sympathetic. More than a few were recent immigrants,

Somali and Yemeni. Instead of chasing the boys, they'd try to reason: "*Please*, boys, you leave now. My boss. He comes."

Rain or shine, inside or out, legal or not, more and more of the city was becoming part of my kids' extended playground.

Mary and I hoped that a new year in a new school—Sean in seventh grade, Leo in sixth—would provide a fresh start, a hard reset.

At Whitman Middle—named for Uncle Walt, that champion of "celebrate myself . . . creeds and schools in abeyance" (school mascot: the Wildcat)—they made new friends quickly. Almost all were skaters, some of whom they'd seen at skate parks. Willful and wily, bullheaded and determined skaters. A combustible stew of them.

There was Max, freckled and funny, who carried a giant backpack filled MacGyver-like with video gear, a flashlight, rope, matches, and glow sticks. "Just in case," he'd say. There was Willem, lanky and happy-go-lucky, always flashing a goofy smirk, usually plugged into an iPod full of hip-hop. He reminded me of a young Ethan Hawke, laconic and sometimes quiet, but capable of surprising you with non-teenager chit-chat—"Hello Mary and Neal, haven't seen you in a while, how was your day?"

And there was Nate, a talented skater and videographer with a mop of dark hair, quiet and thoughtful, sometimes sullen and moody. A lot like Sean. Nate's relationship with Sean reminded me of my friendship with Don. Sean and Nate coaxed and cajoled each other, conspired with each other. In class, they'd try to make eye contact, dare each other to do something silly or naughty. "It's like they're drawn to each other," a counselor later told me.

Other skaters came and went across those first few years in Seattle: Michael, Colman, Cooper, Lysander, Nick, and Nathan. Mary and I got to know them on road trips, at sleepovers, driving them to bus stops and skate parks, listening to their *WTF* backseat conversations . . .

Willem: "Dude, I'm gonna ollie up and big flip out."

Max: "Dope, boy!"

Willem: "Wanna just huff on the six?"

Mary and I shared driving duties with other parents, and the destination requests expanded and diversified. No longer satisfied with Seattle parks and skate spots, they wanted rides to Bellevue, Everett, South Seattle, Mercer Island. Then came the messy transition to public transportation, which brought equal parts relief and fear.

Sean had started riding city buses to school the previous year, and Leo the lawyer began lobbying. "It just makes sense for me to learn how to get around," he said. "Then you and Mom don't have to drive us around!" Though it seemed like we'd only recently let Leo *walk* to school by himself, as usual we slackened the leash.

Though mature for his age (now twelve), in size Leo could still pass for a second grader. When I got a text from him one day—"think i got on wrong bus not sure where i am"—I pictured my little blond guy surrounded by drunken pantswetters, ranting homeless guys. I picked Leo up miles from home, perfectly safe, even a bit exhilarated.

Mary and I were initially uncomfortable letting our Appalachia-softened kids take on Seattle's mass transit, but we were surprised at how many classmates had the freedom to crisscross the city by bus on their own. At first, our plan was to let the boys take the bus to Inner Space. With a toe in that door, they couldn't help themselves. Their sky-blue metro bus passes became their keys to the city, swiping those plastic rectangles like magic wands—*poof,* they're uptown, *poof,* downtown—with or without our permission.

It wasn't just the buses, or the underground parking garages, or the trespassing skate sessions. In every way possible, they kept scheming to move beyond the borders of home, school, and even the skate park, out into the streets— not just neighborhood streets but *city* streets—out past the flimsy perimeter we'd set, into the world on their own.

If my skating had been a pastel-colored tableau, smooth like '70s AM radio, the boys skated like a gray-hued mashup of grunge, punk, and rap, all angsty and illegal . . .

Thighs is the Seattle Police Department, may I speak with the parents of Sean Thompson?"

"What?! Is he *hurt?*" I blurted. "Is he okay? What's wrong!"

The officer assured me that Sean was fine, just a bit too mouthy. He and two friends had turned a neighbor's front stoop into their personal skate park, ripping tricks off his steps until the homeowner came out and told them to scram.

The boys back-talked, the argument escalated, the owner shoved a kid to the ground as another punched 911.

During another after-school roving, my boys and two friends started flinging pinecones at passing cars. A pickup truck slammed to a stop, the driver chased and caught Leo and threw him against a stone wall, yelling, "Don't fucking move or I swear I'll punch you in the face." Sean and another friend ran back to Leo's defense as the driver called the police, who took statements, told the man to just go home, and released my kids.

When the boys explained their side of the story, they were confused by our angry reaction—*You could get hurt! You could get arrested! You could get shot!*

"I *knew* you wouldn't understand," Sean yelled back, which was a new theme, a mantra from our boys: *You just don't get it.* Which was true.

"You never know when it'll be some loon with a *gun*," I said, an ineffective swat at their stalwart righteousness.

"That dude should be locked up," Sean insisted, and Leo vowed to "beat his ass" when he got old enough.

"Leo!" I shouted.

"Dad, relax, I'm just kidding," he said, then turned to Sean, smirking. "Sort of . . ."

There's a skate trick called a "pop-shuvit," which I appreciated for its homophonic declaration of the attitude they'd adopted. That "shove it" stance deepened and darkened as they progressed into the fucked-up morass that is middle school. And, perhaps inevitably, my cherished role as a skate dad diminished.

Lately, Mary began distancing herself from the skate scene. It made her nervous to watch, especially after they mostly stopped wearing helmets. Seattle's skate parks were so noisy and full of boys, rarely a mom in sight. She hated shopping for yet another pair of shoes. So the boys' skating had become more a father-sons endeavor. Until now.

One by one, they began to pluck my fingers off the ledge of parental engagement. They wanted more freedom. Less oversight. Less *dad*, Dad.

They were done with me as driver, videographer, partner. I was demoted. All they really needed from me was bus fare.

By now, the boys seemed to know every skateable piece of concrete, brick, wood, or steel, every off-limits ledge, step, ramp, or rail. They developed an insider's awareness of greater Seattle. Anywhere we went as a family—restaurant, friend's house, doctor's office—it seemed they had been there, or nearby. Years later, Leo and I would ride Amtrak south to Tacoma, and while walking to the train station he showed me the private plaza where they sometimes skated. He explained how they'd make a precarious climb onto a high wall, up and over the spike-topped security fence, and escape the same way if security cornered them. Insider tip: Best way to invite a skater onto your property? Put a fence around it.

Skaters saw things in two shades: skateable, not skate-able. That was their view of the world, and they were con-stantly scanning. I've seen my boys step out of our car in some parking lot or neighborhood and immediately sweep with their eyes and start pointing: *Two-stair over there. Nice ramp. See that pipe?* It was as if they'd developed sonar, the skateable spots glowing like a heat map. I've seen them, in person and on YouTube, skate on, off, up, or over fire hydrants, downed street signs, garbage cans, storefront sandwich boards, shards of plywood, lawn chairs, fence posts, shopping carts, boat ramps, playground slides, tractor trailer beds, and boulders.

They once got busted taking turns skating off a ski-jump-shaped piece of public art at a marina until a woman ran toward them, waving her arms. Max kept his camera rolling, and in his YouTube video he slowed her rant down to a hilarious slo-mo warble. His video ends with the boys taking turns leaping off a pier into Puget Sound.

Did I like the abuse of statuary, and the mocking of its protector? No, I did not. Did I appreciate their exuberantly obnoxious boyishness? Well, as someone who'd been there (and maybe overstayed my time), I knew that pushing the limits and risking my neck and sometimes being a shitbag was what boyhood was all about. The problem was this: as a dad in the age of iPhones and YouTube, I had access to moments that my parents never witnessed. I saw them in the wild, in action. And I was unwilling to look the other way.

Until now, Mary and I had largely adopted our parents' style of governing—as in: not too much.

Home by dinner had been the primary rule in our respective 1970s suburban households. That and go to church and don't get kidnapped. My mother's attitude—"It's your life, NT!"—was a call to self-reliance, a motherly mantra. It shaped me, though not without my exploitations. Mary had similar freedoms. As a skinny, spunky preteen, she rode her horse through the fields surrounding her Illinois farmhouse, and once got tossed to the ground, snapping her collarbone. She was ten.

As newbie parents, Mary and I initially talked about giving our kids the same independence we'd had. Our plan (okay, no real plan, but . . .) went something like: We'll build a fence around our kids, and as long as they stay flapping within the confines of the chicken ranch, they'll have the freedom to make their own decisions. Life will be up to them.

You could say we rejected helicopter parenting long before helicoptering was a thing. Not that we were pushovers. We'd sentenced them to many hours of time-outs and chores, and lately found that taking away their skateboards got their attention—they'd shriek and wail as if we'd hacked off an arm.

Parenting became a series of questions about breaking their spirit, about rigidity versus hands off. The near-daily parental dilemma was: Do we lecture, punish, and pummel them for being who they are, or do we keep them raw and a little wild, and accept the consequences? In tilting toward the latter option, were we too permissive? There were early signs. Maybe we shouldn't have let them watch *The Simpsons* as toddlers, or *South Park* soon after, or those less-than-appropriate movies. An aunt once shrieked, "You let them watch *The Godfather?*" Leo would later recall the time we tried watching *Fast Times at Ridgemont High* together, until they asked us to turn it off—"That was definitely a questionable decision," he said.

For the most part, though, we saw no upside to shielding them. And underparenting seemed to work just fine when they were smart-ass tykes. But now? In middle school? Our free-range "it's your life" approach had become a blank check to two preteen skaters with bus passes.

After watching *The Blind Side* with a gang of friends, Sean and Leo took the bus to Nate's house for a sleepover. I talked to Leo by phone after the movie—he was weepy because he'd left his skateboard at the movie theater—then Mary and I went to bed.

Hours later, the phone rang. I grabbed the alarm clock: 2:30 A.M. A ringing telephone after midnight was never good news.

"Dad? Dad! Daddy, my *daddy*—DADDY!" It was Leo, crying and in a blubbery panic, but I couldn't understand what he was saying.

"Leo what's wrong? Where are you?" He couldn't answer, bawling and then yelling, "No, no, *no*! Why, why, *why?*"

My heart clenched, my throat choked, and my brain sprinted to its darkest place: Sean is hurt. Sean is *dead*.

Mary found the other handset and took control. She asked Leo who else was there, then told him to give the phone to Nate, who was also crying.

"Nate, what's going on?"

Between his sobs he managed to tell us that Sean was missing: "He left an hour ago. We can't find him!"

Mary dialed Nate's parents while I ran to my car, planning to drive to Nate's house. But the windshield was covered with fucking frost. As I frantically scraped and cursed, bloodying my gloveless knuckles, I looked up to see the ghostly image of a small person walking slowly down the sidewalk. As it came closer, I recognized . . .

"Sean? SEAN! Oh my god, oh Jesus Christ, are you okay? What the . . . ?"

I raced over and scooped him into my arms, crying and yelling stupidly out to Mary and the neighborhood, "I've got him, he's here, he's home!"

Sean seemed stunned, and I was terrified to ask how he'd gotten here. Creep in a van? Had someone, you know . . . *touched* him? Was he *hurt*?

What happened was this: Sean and Nate had gotten into a heated argument, so Sean just left, started walking in the direction he hoped was home. For five miles. Along busy four-lane streets. Past bus stops and through crappy neighborhoods. For nearly two hours.

By now Nate's mom had reached Mary, and when she brought Leo home she filled in the rest. How the boys woke her up to tell her Sean was gone, how she drove around looking for him, assuming he'd be wandering through the neighborhood, how she began to fear the worst, how Leo and Nate convinced themselves that Sean was dead.

Inside our house, I found Sean in the bathroom, staring

at himself in the mirror with a satisfied look that I read as pride. A look that seemed to say: *I did it.*

The next night at dinner, Sean asked—a little too curiously—what'd happen if Mary and I died and he was orphaned. Could he wander off into the world, sad but free?

"If you guys weren't around I wouldn't feel the need to be good. I wouldn't *care,*" he said, warming to the fantasy. "I'd just leave here and go wherever I wanted and do whatever I wanted. I'd sleep on trains and in parks and go from town to town. It wouldn't matter what I did, and nobody would know or care.

"I mean . . . I wonder if there are people who live like that?" said our son.

"Yeah," Mary told him. "Homeless people."

continued to believe skating was good for my kids, that it divulged secrets about an increasingly complex and volatile planet. Even with all the troubling flare-ups, I remained convinced that skating honed an awareness of real people and real places, of race, ethnicity, and even economics. Mary and I, consciously or not, sent our kids a message that figuring some of *those* things out mattered as much as calculus and the Constitution. My thinking went: by learning to navigate a city of strangers—by bus, foot, and board—they were learning about life on the streets, developing a sense of direction, learning conflict-resolution skills, sharpening their independence, and their courage.

One night, I ran my fingers across highlighted and underlined quotes in my battered copy of Emerson's "Self-Reliance," offering some needed but unsteady comfort. "Is it so bad, then, to be misunderstood?" . . . "imitation is suicide"..."trust thyself." As someone who'd strived to embrace Emerson's call to the genuine, misunderstood, unapologetic life, how could I not let my kids strive for the same? Uncle Ralph might've frowned upon certain aspects of the skate life, but still: "My life is not an apology . . . It is for itself and not for a spectacle."

And yet, it also seemed too soon for us to have lost *control*. Every day brought a new conflict, a new ticked-off caller, and more noisy punishments. It was never their fault. The grown-ups never understood.

One night it was Mike from Inner Space, *again*. The boys had gotten shooed away from the "Adobe steps," as they now called them, then snuck under the fence of a storage facility, whose security guard gave chase. That was followed by a round of ding-dong-ditch through the neighborhood, prompting calls to Inner Space from angry neighbors.

Mike said he and the other managers were starting to get pissed off at the escalating bullshit. The boys had been causing all kinds of ruckus. They'd been banned from Subway and other local stores, and Mike was tempted to start banning them from Inner Space.

"I'd been meaning to tell you, but I didn't want to cause trouble," he said. "I keep warning them not to be total assholes. It's just not cool."

I told Mike I was surprised that they'd turned their defiance on him, on their skate park, on their own kind. He just sighed.

"Man, when a gang of them gets together it just spins out of control. They just go *crazy*."

As I drove toward Inner Space, Sean called me in tears. He was standing outside a ding-dong-ditch victim's house. In the background I heard the guy yelling—he wanted Sean and Nate to come inside while he called the cops. "No!" I screamed. "Do NOT go inside! Run, Sean, *run*!" But he inexplicably handed his phone to the man, to whom I apologized profusely and told him, "I'm on my way to get the boys. I'll take them far from your home, I swear." I was becoming an expert apologist. *Sorry, sorry, sorry.*

Having fully slammed into the reality of what it meant to *really* be a skater, crappy phone conversations began invading our nights, a fugly new phase, a family psychosis. It was as if a soccer mom discovered that having a talented soccer kid required an occasional carjacking. But we'd given our boys so much freedom it now seemed impossible to put the genie back. Our decision to not *over*parent was taunting us with the consequences of *under*parenting.

Even worse: we unintentionally rewarded bad behavior. For reasons I didn't fully understand, our family kept returning to skate parks, lured by some voice that spoke to us all.

For Sean's thirteenth birthday, we took Amtrak down to Portland. On the ride south, we let our boys and Nate explore the train as Mary and I sipped beers in the café car. Then a grouchy conductor announced, "Would the parents of three unattended juveniles please . . ." They'd snuck into a vacant sleeper car suite and helped themselves to showers.

In Portland, after checking into our hotel, we caught the light rail out to Ed Benedict Skatepark. Nate had previously injured his ankle skating and was wearing an orthopedic boot. He kept trying to skate with the boot but finally bailed and pulled out his video camera. The clips from that afternoon—Nate's and mine—tell a story of boys losing themselves at a skate park, each skating a solo performance but connected to a bigger entity, a multitentacled organism.

The sun slowly sets. The park gets crowded. Overhead lights flicker on, off, on. Sean keeps trying the same series of tricks, again and again. Skaters call it a "line"—like a dancer working a routine. His intended line: drop down a ramp, ollie onto a mani-pad, then manual (i.e. wheelie) across the platform, then pop-shuvit, then kickflip off the ledge. After multiple, curse-filled attempts, Sean finally nails it, and Leo and Nate swoop in for congratulatory high fives, fist bumps, hang-loose surfer shaka waggles.

But the video segment that I'd later watch obsessively, sometimes tearfully—to remind myself there was a *point* to all of it—was a thirty-second slice of my YouTube clip of Leo trying to ollie down a tricky three-stair. First try: Leo accelerates toward the steps but pulls up shy, daunted. Second try: he clears the stairs—at least ten feet in length, and nearly a four-foot drop—but lands too hard. His board spins out, his butt and helmet smack concrete, he screams and rolls as skaters swerve around him. Third try: similar wipeout, feet and legs folding under his ass, more screams. Four and five: getting closer, but he scrapes his hands on number four and nearly gets smeared by a BMX biker on number five.

And then . . . Leo pushes off hard with his right foot, accelerates, crouches low, pops a huge ollie, soars through the air, arms out like wings, sticks the landing, and pumps his fists. He kick-turns back and Sean is waiting with giddy high fives, as if Leo had just homered in two runs. Nate, laughing, hands him a bottle of water and drapes him in a bro hug. On the light rail ride back downtown, I videotape the three of them, grinning and smirking, like they've just gotten away with something, like they're sharing a secret.

The soundtrack I'd added to my video, from Spoon, meshed nicely: "It was the longest day that I'd ever known . . . Oh, life could be so fair. Let it go on and on."

My sons were learning to fly. I understood that. And I *wanted* them to fly, though not too much. I also wanted them to *comply*. Why couldn't they do both?

Though they'd become defiant and disdainful at school and at home, on the Internet—out in the world they'd created—they were downright joyful.

YouTube had become their canvas, their gallery of glee. Many of the skaters carried at least a Flip camera, and a few, like Nate, lugged backpacks full of digital or tape cameras, tripods, fish-eye lenses, and handheld stabilizer rigs. They were all proficient with video editing software—at least iMovie or, like Nate, the more advanced Final Cut.

My boys' core crew through middle school remained Max and Nate, each with his own YouTube channel, and Willem, who was the leading man in many of the other boys' videos.

Sean and Leo each had a YouTube channel, and they usually shared filming and editing duties until Leo, over time, edged ahead to become the more devoted videographer. He made dozens of videos, especially after we superglued a fisheye lens onto his Flip camcorder. He began proudly adding credits, "Filmed and Edited by Leo Thompson," crafting birthday edits, basement edits, backyard edits. One video was titled "fun . . . fun . . . fun . . . fun . . . fun . . . fun." Another: "Sunday Funday."

My own videos, like "Daddy Day Camp"—scenes from a day with Leo, Sean, and Willem on Mercer Island—quickly grew outdated and blah, since I was no longer part of their adventurous, city-roving crew. I'd check their YouTube channels and snoop, watching them rolling and flying through our soggy city, skating at ATM plazas, fast-food joints, high schools, beneath the convention center, among the crowds at waterfront tourist spots. They'd tumble into bushes, sprawl onto sidewalks, take turns soaring off the backs of flatbed trucks. They'd chug grape sodas and scarf tacos or burgers. They'd confront hand-waving security guards.

I became a YouTube voyeur, watching their personalities and young manhoods take shape, watching the baby fat melt and sharpen. To this day, you can see them all start to mature in videos like "key bank parking garage," "willem x construction site," "leo is stupid," "sean gets robbed," "nate hurts ass," "crazy old lady," "20 bucks," and one starring Max titled, accurately, "smashing my balls." Subtitle: "a quick rail sesh ending in pain." The entire dialogue: "Oh! Oh, fuck! *Ow!*"

The contrast between their expressive skating-on-YouTube life and their follow-the-rules school life was stark.

Sean, in particular, resisted academic expectations. Scolding e-mails from teachers became a constant reminder of our parental impotence. "Sean is missing a lot of our class daydreaming" . . . "Just an FYI, Sean got up and walked out of science today" . . . "refused to suit up for gym."

Mary and I rarely worried about his intellect. He scored well on standardized tests and, if he chose to make an effort, impressed teachers, especially on writing assignments.

But we did worry about his commitment. One teacher found a cluster of completed worksheets crammed into his desk, as if turning them in would've been a surrender. We also worried about his happiness. Which led us to seek professional opinions.

A child psychologist gave Sean a battery of tests, none of them conclusive. In short: he's a smart kid but inattentive and poorly organized, outwardly headstrong but lacking confidence. The psychologist dropped a few acronyms, suggested ADHD meds, but offered no real diagnosis except: "He should be doing better in school." Which we already knew.

Still, we tried a few suggested treatments: talk therapy, acupuncture, squishy stress-reduction fidget toys. We researched attention-deficit drugs, and reluctantly agreed with a doctor's suggestion to try Ritalin, then quickly regretted it.

One morning Sean sat at his desk, dreaming about kickflips. He later told us the half dose of Ritalin was making him jumpy and he got stuck in a loop and became obsessed with the question: Which pair of skate shoes was best for kickflips? He couldn't stop himself, so after lunch he skipped out and came home to practice in our basement, trying on different shoes, measuring the scraped-rubber factor of each toe, watching YouTube videos for guidance.

"I was trying to get the *flick* just right," he told me, as if it was a legit excuse for truancy. "I was trying to understand the physics of it."

I forget whether we punished Sean by taking away his board or banning YouTube or both, but I do remember his rage. "Middle school isn't learning," he argued. "If I was learning something useful I wouldn't mind, but they aren't teaching me anything, so why should I spend my time on it?"

We quit the Ritalin and tried a new therapist, a gruff New Yorker who hit it off with Sean and told us he just needed to grow up. Which we already knew.

Sean came home one day with an A on a test, but he seemed embarrassed by my enthusiastic reaction, as if he'd been unfaithful to his defiant side. He skulked down the alley, took a bus to skate somewhere alone.

"I only want to be with my friends and have fun and skateboard," Sean later said-slash-yelled. "That's all I want to do, just skateboard. That's it!"

A school counselor e-mailed a group of parents to report an "incident" in the appropriately named after-school "Wildcat Den." She'd "witnessed" a few boys using some toy to pretend-smoke a bong. She said it was "clear to me that they had some experience with it." Mary and I dutifully grounded our sons, made them come home after school for a week, surly and sour. But . . . were they really so naughty? Were the constant reminders from counselors and teachers—*There's something wrong with your kid!*—really helping them?

Mary was getting impatient with the complaints and the blame-the-parent approach to difficult boys. We'd witnessed plenty of slogan-backed support for girls, empowerment programs for science, math, and coding. But for academically disengaged skate boys? The only slogan seemed to be "sit down and knock it off!"

"I just don't understand it," Mary said one night, after a scolding e-mail from a school security guard named Rose. "Why isn't someone *encouraging* them? It pisses me off."

Other times, we'd flog ourselves . . . "What are we doing wrong?" Mary asked, during a rare moment of pessimism. "Are we losing the battle?"

Mary was an efficient and decisive thinker—quick to judge, quick to conviction, quick to move on. I was more of an either-or guy, and an occasional handwringer. Like . . . On the one hand, I viewed the middle grades as a confusing twilight zone, just past the coddling of singsongy grade school yet just shy of the teenage freedoms of high school. That meant teachers were dealing with kids in flux, juiced by hormones. I wanted to believe the teachers were devoted to all students, not just the compliant and hardworking ones, not just the girls, who were clearly more sensible and obliging than their immature and annoying male peers. I wanted to trust the system.

On the other hand, Sean's science teacher—who once told me she had to google some of the words she heard the boys using—relied on Hollywood for her lesson plans, showing disaster movies to discuss global warming, for example. The same teacher would quote from her union contract, telling students, "I'm not required to do that."

Fake bongs were presumably on the not-required list. But I couldn't quite muster Mary's indignation. I felt blamed and ashamed, irrationally guilty for my kids' behavior.

Meanwhile, Sean had devised his own personal lesson plan. Call it Ghetto 101.

He'd become obsessed with gritty, urban America, and could spend an hour or two researching slums and inner-city housing projects via Google Earth and Wikipedia. He'd watch YouTube videos of not only skaters but graffiti artists, rappers, and street-fight beat downs. He frequented sites like Vice and WorldStarHipHop, known as the "CNN of the ghetto." In no time, Sean could list America's most dangerous cities, the worst low-income projects, national crime stats, and the murder rates of Baltimore, New York, Chicago, and Miami.

Though Seattle was a blindingly white city, through skating my boys had made friends of color, and Sean had become especially attuned to any perceived race-based slights. When a teacher disciplined a Filipino friend, Sean muttered *rac-*

ist. When asked to repeat it, Sean looked the teacher in the eye and accused him of picking on darker-skinned students, earning a trip to the principal. When a Boys & Girls Club counselor punished another friend, Sean sniped, "Oh, because he's *black?*" The counselor sent Sean to the director's office, but Sean slipped out a side door and walked home in a huff. Sensitivity to injustice and inequity was seemingly stitched into his DNA. Back in North Carolina, on a road trip, he'd refused to join Mary and Leo for a walking tour of Duke University's campus, claiming it was home to drunk lacrosse players, "racists and rapists."

I appreciated this affinity for the underdog, which reminded me of the lessons my sister had taught me about acceptance and compassion. Many of the boys' skate friends shared a sense of justice and righteousness, which I admired, but with trepidation. By skating the streets of Seattle, riding buses far and wide, they certainly witnessed more city grit than some kids their age, crossing paths with the homeless and the downtrodden, panhandlers and alley lurkers.

Mary and I tried to put a positive spin on some of it. Maybe they'll study urban economics? Become social workers? I'd think back on Sean's essay about skating as "nondiscriminatory," open to everyone regardless of "race, age, gender, size, strength, social skills, background, education, sexual orientation," as he'd put it. Then again, if inclusion was a core skater value, where was the empathy for hardworking teachers and counselors and cops? Sean sometimes seemed conflicted by his own inclinations.

"I only like to do things if they lead to something else,"

he said one day after school. "But if I'm only going to work at McDonald's the only thing I need is a clean criminal record." This comment came before an epic night of homework battles. Sean had four worksheets to complete but first started watching a movie, then *South Park*, then skate videos. I kept shutting off his screens—"What's the point?" he complained—and only after I threatened to take away his board did he finally sit down and finish his work. In ten minutes.

The next day I read an article about a father who was acquitted of assault after dragging his teen son by the hair for refusing to do homework. I actually felt bad for the guy.

Later that week, I found Sean sitting in a corner of the basement after school, staring into the waffle-pattern sole of a skate shoe, quietly despondent. He told me he was starting to worry about high school, and college, and a job . . . He was screwing up middle school, he said, as he started tapping his forehead with the shoe. He was worried he would screw up high school, too—*tap, tap*—and end up working at a gas station. He said he wanted to be homeschooled. He said he wanted to be in a spaceship.

"Sometimes I just wish I could be in outer space," he said.

"You mean, like, an astronaut?" I asked.

"No, not a NASA spaceship. A UFO. I want to be on a different planet. A bigger planet. I want to be with aliens."

He began hitting himself harder with the shoe, and I sat down beside him on the concrete floor, put my arm around him, gently taking the shoe away.

Finally, he said, "I just want to be your little Seany-shoo

again. I want to be a little guy. I just want to live here with you and Mumslo."

"Um, forever?" I asked.

"I dunno."

"Well, you'll probably change your mind about that."

"Maybe."

Meanwhile, as Sean wrestled with who he was and who he wanted to be—vagabond or alien, skater or little boy—Leo was going through his own weird boy shit.

Home life had devolved into a messy morass, and the strife was affecting Leo, who mostly wanted everyone to play their part and get along and be *happy*. The kid who once wished for the whole world to be Hawaii was now anxious and edgy. He'd developed a gag-like mouth twitch that looked like a mother bird choking up prechewed food for her chicks. He poked and picked at his mouth and nose, which led to an infection, and trips to a dermatologist. He started visiting a Chinese acupuncturist for his mouth twitch and stress.

To be clear, Leo could be a teacher-taunting smart aleck, too—and would catch up to Sean in that department—but he at least *tried* to play the role of middle schooler. He even had a girlfriend, and they'd walk the halls adorably holding hands, until the day he came home crying. I was in the kitchen and saw him coming up the alley, a stomp-walk that meant something was wrong. When he opened the back gate and I saw his face, I knew it was trouble. He broke down and told me how she'd dumped him—by text.

"I know it's just, like, sixth grade, and it shouldn't matter," he said, in tears as we sat at the kitchen table. "But she was just, like, *really* cool and I just don't *get* it."

I tried to comfort him but realized Leo's preteen boyhood had become a bummer: brother falling apart, parents always yelling at him, brother yelling back, parents sometimes yelling at each other . . . And why are they always talking about money and homework and chores and "life"? Why can't we all just be frickin' *happy*?

Truth is, some nights we could be a family freak show. I surely didn't help by letting the stress of my freelance writing career, its sporadic income, and my ineffectual parenting all escalate into a noisy scrum. And I didn't help anyone by self-medicating with bourbon.

I'd been working on a new book, but not fast enough, so I'd get testy when I wasn't writing well, then pour an afternoon beer or whiskey to help squeeze out a few more words. I never got *drunk*-drunk, though one night I crossed the line and in a boozy snit shattered a cocktail glass that Mary had given me for my birthday. I didn't actually mean to throw it *at* my wife, but I was flailing my arms, arguing some long-forgotten point, and the whiskey glass flew in her direction and smashed against the fridge. Mary gave me a cold, hard look that I'd never seen before. She was furious, and a little scared. I tried to explain that it was an accident, but she wouldn't let me off so easy.

"You threw a *glass* at me," she said.

Usually, the most stable one at dinner was Leo. No wonder he preferred hanging at Max's house, where, he'd tell us, the parents read in the dining room while the kids played video games in the next room, a fat dog in the mix, "But they're all *together*." At Max's, Leo and Max romped like *boy*-boys, silly and dorky, in no hurry to grow up. "They're a real family," he told Mary one night during one of their neighborhood walks. "We never do *anything* as a family."

Lately, I'd watched Leo veer back and forth between skate friends and new friends his own age, including nonskaters. He also began testing some radical ideas, like studying and doing homework, and even trying new hobbies. After rejecting music lessons years earlier he decided to try guitar, then switched to drums. Then he joined a basketball league — bravely, I thought, since he was the shortest kid on his team.

One Friday night Leo went to a trampoline place with a new friend's church group. Except for weddings and funerals, we hadn't exposed the boys to much religion, so when the church van dropped him off at the end of the night, I was curious . . .

"Did you *pray*?" I asked Leo as we drove home.

"No," he said. "We just bounced."

9

As we trudged up the rocky path toward the volcanic cone of Diamond Head, only two in our sweaty pack of sun-pinked tourists lugged the unnecessary baggage of a skateboard.

Sean and Leo had insisted on bringing their boards on the climb, through tunnels and up ladders, in hopes of finding a secret off-limits skate spot they'd seen in videos. Based on our years of failing to get the boys to hike with us, the boards were an acceptable compromise. We didn't find their spot, but on the descent they managed to skate the final stretch of paved pathway, slaloming through startled tourists as I obnoxiously snapped photos.

The next day, as most Honolulu visitors sunned themselves on Waikiki Beach or snorkeled or surfed, we were driving the back roads of Diamond Head, looking for that skate spot. Sean saw a weed-choked lot and a crime-scene set of concrete steps that he recognized . . .

"Stop here, I think we're close," he said.

So many family trips ended up like this, venturing way off beaten paths, down alleys and into creepy city armpits, looking for renegade parks or off-limits skate spots, with little to guide us but my kids' memory of YouTube scenes and some cues from Google Maps. They were like backcountry skiers—the real fun happened out of bounds. So we parked the rental car and hiked up the inland ass-crack of Diamond Head, not another soul in sight, along a hint of a pathway, littered and glittery with busted bottles, past the chains and NO TRESPASSING signs, Sean and Leo insisting we were getting close.

We emerged onto an expanse of jagged, multitiered, graffiti-covered concrete, and the boys were instantly Disney-like euphoric. Far from home, impelled by instinct and parental dereliction, they'd found their spot, the foundation of a demolished school now decorated by orphaned couches, heaps of trash, a burned-out motorcycle frame. It was absurd, but I was excited, too. Mary left the three of us and went for a long run as I pulled out our gear—cameras, tripod, homemade video stabilizer, etc.—and we got to work.

For two hours, the boys skated themselves sweaty, ollie-ing the wrecked motorcycle, 360-ing over chunks of concrete, kickflipping off ledges and over scrap lumber as I took photos and shot video. The sun began to slump and Mary did postrun squats and stretches and I took final portraits of the boys posing beside a piss-stained couch, Leo in his yellow Hawaiian shirt and Sean in his stretched-out STILL LIVIN T-shirt, downtown Honolulu shimmering beneath them. I realized, once again, that we were a weird-ass family.

Leo had partly inspired the trip, with his call for more family unity and —in a rebuttal against Sean's ghetto fixation, and against rainy Seattle—his hopeful visions of tropical paradise. I had encouraged Hawaii as a destination because it'd allow me to indulge my growing curiosity about the origins of the *board* that had come to dominate our days.

Close to finishing my latest book (a biography of the eccentric, world-traveling cartoonist, Robert "Believe It or Not" Ripley), I'd started researching the history of surfing, the sport that sired skating. Surfboard, skateboard, snowboard, they all seemed to lure boys like mine into a certain lifestyle—or maybe they were totems of a lifestyle such boys already craved. But what was it about the board itself, I wondered, that *plank*? Was it a primal reminder of some ancient weapon? Undeniably dick-shaped, was there something sexual about surfing, snowboarding, and skating? Was the board an extra phallus? Were the boys all overcompensating?

I couldn't exactly ask my kids and their friends my dumb questions, so I sought clues elsewhere.

I took surf lessons on Waikiki from a tubby instructor named Pat, who danced across his board like Fred Astaire. I checked out the beautifully carved, sensually shaped, century-old wooden boards at the Bishop Museum, and learned how Christian missionaries' disapproval of Hawaiian surfing had pushed it to the brink of extinction. I read about Jack London's 1907 visit, and his still-apt description of a young surfer dude: "upright on his board, carelessly poised, a young god bronzed with sunburn." I bought books about the godfather of modern surfing, Duke Kahanamoku, of whom a fellow surfer said: "He had an inner tranquility. It was as if he knew something we didn't know." And I reread Tom Wolfe's *The Pump House Gang*, which captured the darker side of board riding—the drinking and drugs, the self-destructive ennui of the California surf lifestyle that begat skating.

Revisiting Wolfe's classic made me realize that bored Seattle boys on boards were, in spirit and in action, the same kids Wolfe had described a half century earlier, teens on the fringe of society, burdened by the "hassle of the adolescent, the feeling that he is being prodded into adulthood on somebody else's terms."

I'd also started reading books by and about Tony Hawk, Laird Hamilton, and other skaters and surfers. I learned that Hawk's parents had given him tons of freedom as a kid and "never yanked the normal parent leash," as he put it. He didn't like team sports, or school, and he quit violin lessons at an early age. His father was his "personal chauffeur" who "logged hundreds of miles every weekend driving me from park to park." Skate parks became his "family room," his "clubhouse"—"the Elks Club for kids with scabs." Like Leo, he was often the smallest kid and often felt like an outsider, a distracted doodler, "detached from the normal crowd."

I recognized my kids and their friends in the words of Hawk and other skate pioneers. Christian Hosoi: "I always loved doing whatever I wanted." Tony Alva: "Our attitude was like, 'We skate—fuck you!'" Rodney Mullen: "What skater doesn't feel like an outsider? It's a collection of people who don't belong in collections."

My reading and research taught me this much: riding a board had historically been something to be ashamed of and/or defensive about. For centuries people had been telling board riders to knock it off and get a job. The missionaries scolded Hawaiian surfers to cut up their boards and make desks. And I loved the story of the teacher who told Hawk that by "defying authority" and following a "path of disobedience" his future looked bleak. Instead, the millionaire skate entrepreneur wrote: "Skateboarding saved me."

Then again, the ties between surfing and skating meant little to my kids. Nursing bad memories of a family attempt at surfing in Oregon, they'd declined to join me for my Waikiki surf lessons. Afterward, as I lay baking beside Mary on a towel, we watched the boys walking toward us, two pale and sweaty Seattle kids trudging across this famous beach—a beach that could be called the womb of skate culture. Instead of barefoot and shirtless, they toted their boards as their skate shoes kicked up puffs of white sand.

"Coming to join us?" I asked. "Go for a swim?"

"Nah," Leo said, grabbing a water bottle and downing half of it in three chugs.

They'd been doing tricks off curbs and sewer pipes in a nearby parking lot and were on their way to another spot.

"Going skatin'," Sean said.

Surfers are beautiful boys with buff torsos. They're tanned

and slick with seawater, pure and wise and zen, even when they're badass, like Patrick Swayze's "Bodhi" in *Point Break* (one of our family faves). And snowboarders? They're high-flying daredevils, medal-winning Olympians, as are their two-boarded skier brethren.

But skaters? They're street rats. My kids took pride in doing the less obvious, like spending a sunny day in the frying pan of a parking lot while others lounged at the beach.

On their boards, I realized, my kids felt whole and in control. Among like-minded skaters, they felt protected and accepted. They'd found something on a skateboard and among skaters that just made *sense*. As Hawk put it, they'd found "a secret club the rest of the world didn't know about."

What nagged at me was this: What if their secret club pulled them too far afield? What about their relationship with *the rest of the world?*

In the spring of 2010, three young men, recent grads of our local high school, were killed in an early-morning car wreck. They'd been speeding in the rain when the driver lost control and slammed into a signpost outside the Taco Time.

Two months later, a lightbulb in an apartment closet torched a foam mattress and fire raced through the home of Sean's classmate Joey, a sweet, skinny thirteen-year-old whose family had immigrated from Ethiopia. Joey, two sisters, a cousin, and an aunt all died. It was the deadliest Seattle fire in decades, and the tragedy devastated Whitman Middle School. Instead of giddiness to start the summer, the school hallways hosted tearful scenes of wracked and wounded friends and cries of "Joey!"

Days later, teachers led students onto the soccer field for a memorial service, arranging them in a big circle. Once everyone had joined hands, boys and girls started praying, then weeping, then wailing. Sean called me in tears. "It's horrible, Dad. Guys I'd never imagined crying were bawling their eyes out. Girls were screaming. Just *horrible*."

Sean and Leo left school and hopped a city bus, along with Willem and Nate. I asked Sean to put Leo on, who said, "I just can't be alone right now. I just want to be with my friends, so we can all stay close and just be together." I knew what bus they were on, and I knew where they were headed: Inner Space. The number 28 bus rolled right past Joey's home, where classmates and neighbors gathered beside flowers and handwritten signs—JOEY, WE WILL NEVER FORGET YOU   that had bloomed outside the charred apartment building.

I thought back to the tragedies of my youth: classmates and friends killed in car wrecks, felled by cancer or suicide. None of that, not even my mother's or sister's deaths, prepared me for helping my kids confront such inexplicable loss as Joey and his family and those three young men. I felt so ill-equipped. This was the boys' first up-close exposure to death, and I worried I was blowing a chance to impart some parental wisdom. I wanted to help, but there was nothing I could say. All I could do was hug them, which was really more for me.

For real comfort, the boys turned to skating, and mourned

with their friends. Skating was their vigil, and the skate park a place of commiseration. Inside subterranean Inner Space, amid rap music and clackety skate sounds, they were in a safe zone. The skate park had become "more than just a place to skate," as Hawk once said.

Leo created an "R.I.P. Joseph" video, a montage of skate tricks in tribute to their lost friend. In his YouTube description he wrote: "no one deserves to die at 13. we all love you and miss you. . . . . .good bye Joseph." For the music Leo chose an appropriately sober rap song by Bone Thugs-N-Harmony, which captured his state of mind . . .

> You know, don't nothing come easy
> You gotta try real real hard
> I've tried hard, but I guess I gotta try harder.

Weeks later, death came to our family, three years minus a day past my mom's death. Mary's dad had been sick for months, but he'd downplayed the seriousness of the condition that was constricting his weakened heart. He died calmly in an easy chair, late one night at home in North Carolina, with Mary, her mom, and her sister by his side.

At Bill's funeral, after his sister gave the eulogy, she asked if anyone else wanted to say a few words, and Sean jumped out of his seat and strode to the front of the church. He seemed tense, agitated, and Mary and I exchanged "uh-oh" looks. But then . . .

"I just can't believe he's gone," Sean began, his anger melting. "He was so . . . so *fit*. So active. So alive. He has this . . . *essence.*"

Sean talked about how Grandpa Bill always kept busy, how he and Grandma Pauline always had fun, gardened and fished and hiked and threw parties, cooked great food and traveled the world and really, really *lived*. They had shown him what it meant to be alive, he said.

"Why did he have to die?" Sean asked us all. "*Why?*"

He sat down beside Leo, who stared at him for a moment, then leaned his head on Sean's shoulder.

Once again, my kids found some refuge on the board. The day after the funeral, we took the boys to a skate park south of Asheville, and in the dimming summer dusk, beneath banks of spotlights, we watched with clenched jaws as Leo made numerous attempts at ollie-ing down an eight-stair set. Without a helmet.

Surfers often refer to wave height in relation to their body: chest high, overhead, double-overhead. Though some classmates were already man-size, twelve-year-old Leo was still stretching toward five feet, with a blond-topped baby face that could pass for nine. So the height of this eight-stair was decidedly overhead. From the platform above the stairs, Leo propelled himself to full speed, crouched down low, then popped off the top step and into the air. He soared out over the concrete descent, the board glued improbably to his feet, a bold rejection of physics—and of safety. Instead of landing gracefully he crashed violently, tumbling and rolling like in those old Road Runner cartoons.

The boys had skated there the previous day and made a

few quick friends, who nicknamed Leo "Seattle." A few of them now gathered, a mix of white, black, and Hispanic, to watch Leo fling himself off the ledge. They began chanting, "Seattle! Seattle!" but Leo kept missing his landing, scratching and bruising himself, then stalking angrily back to the lineup. We'd lunched at a Mexican restaurant, and I could feel the *pollo asado* churning in my gut. I felt torn between intervening and letting it play out.

So many times, at so many parks and skate spots, I'd watched them attempt the same trick ten, twenty, *fifty* times. They'd developed their own version of Samuel Beckett's oft-quoted advice: "try again, fail again, fail better." My kids' take: fall, fall again, fall better.

By now, I'd grown to admire skating's try-harder credo, its cozy relationship with failure, the embrace of which was built into the whole system. The only way a skater improved was by courting bodily harm, living in his danger zone, pushing to the edge of his abilities, failing, then doing it again. (Search YouTube for "skate fails" and you can easily waste an hour in a state of perma-cringe.) As someone who'd become more risk-averse with age, I often witnessed my kids' exploration of their mortal limits in a clutch of fear and awe.

Mary's sister looked on wide-eyed—"I can't believe you're letting him do this without a helmet!"

It was hard to explain to others that it was out of our hands, as was the cursing . . . "Sonofa-*bitch*!" Leo yelled.

We'd seen this side of Leo before—determined, angry, focused. Like the day he taught himself to ride a bike, on his sixth birthday, rolling and falling and screaming down the sloped, snow-splotched backyard of our North Carolina house for what seemed hours until he could finally pedal around proudly.

Thankfully, it took Leo only a few more tumbles before he nailed his big eight-stair ollie. With his arms up and out like wings, his hands turned down like a gymnast's, he looked like an airborne version of the Karate Kid in that crane-kick pose. For what seemed like half a minute, my son was flying.

Leo's grit earned respectful board slaps and high fives from the other kids, which he accepted with a taut smile. He also earned a few battle scars, his knees, wrists, and elbows road-rashed from the concrete. Leo later explained how and why, despite his many flights over surfaces that could tear his skin and break his bones, he'd never gotten seriously hurt, at least thus far.

In short, he said: "You learn how to fall."

I thought about that sentiment as I watched Mary struggle to accept the loss of her father, watched the boys mourn the loss of a man with whom they'd spent the first half of their lives. I later found a school essay Leo wrote, describing Bill as "one of the most important people in my life. He was a leader, a role model, MY role model." Leo wrote about the day he and Sean had been skating in the backyard when I got the call from Mary, how I'd called them inside to tell them their grandfather was dead.

"That's when I started to cry," Leo wrote. "I cupped my hands over my face and let them fill up. How could he be gone? I wish I could have seen him one more time to say good-bye and tell him how much I loved him and that I would never EVER forget him."

10

After my mom died, it was down to just the men of our family: Jeff in New Jersey, running his own construction company; my dad in Florida, working for the government, flirting with retirement but not ready to stop earning; and me on the opposite coast, thousands of miles away. We lived on three of America's four corners.

We'd call or send Christmas cards but often forgot each other's birthdays. We'd see each other every year or two, but I nursed a deep guilt for not keeping us closer. I did what I could to sustain our long-distance relationship, including a Gmail calendar reminder to "Call Phil" every Sunday at three. (Success rate: roughly 40 percent.)

For as long as I could remember, I'd called him Phil. Or *Jughead*, the nickname he'd earned in high school. My mom called him that, too. Along the way I'd simply stopped calling him *dad*. We'd rarely been a buddy-buddy team, at least not for many years. We didn't swap dirty jokes or stock tips or, god forbid, talk politics. We never said I love you or I miss you. I sometimes worried that Maura and my mom had been the heart and soul of our family, that without them the three boys were a bit untethered.

Yet over the years, nudged in no small part by the mutual ache of losing Maura and then my mom, Phil and I had managed to find some common ground: music, cars, beer, a little bit of sports, a mutual appreciation for Jack Daniel's and kin. And now: the shared experience of fathering two coltish boys.

As the parenting of Sean and Leo got more complicated I'd sometimes ask him, *How did you guys do it?* He rarely had much to offer, claiming not to remember a whole lot about me and Jeff as teens. My theory? He'd blocked most of that shit out. I also think he enjoyed watching me twist. He sometimes just laughed at my latest story of teen nonsense.

But I worried about my sons having a spotty connection to my father, especially once they were down to just two grandparents. So I came up with a plan to lure Phil to Seattle and, along with Sean and Leo, to re-create a portion of an infamous road trip our family had taken in the summer of 1979, just before I started high school.

An engineer and mechanically inclined tinkerer, his hands often dirty with engine grease from weekend sports car projects, my dad had spent months converting a Vietnam-era army ambulance into a camper. The drab beast, a galumphing furnace that smelled of burning oil and grinding gears, chugged along at fifty-two miles an hour, the big red cross on our flanks collecting amused stares as we drove from New Jersey up into Canada, down into Michigan, Wisconsin, the Dakotas, Wyoming, and Colorado.

In those pre-iPod days, my brother and I whined and wrestled and slept fitfully in the broiling back cabin. Vacationers gawked as our *M*A*S*H*-style vehicle juddered into KOA campsites. We explored the Badlands, Mount Rushmore, Yosemite, the Grand Canyon, and camped under the stars deep inside Utah's crimson canyons. We also broke down twice, and during the slingshot drive back east spent two days stuck beside the highway as my dad hitchhiked to Amarillo for an engine part. It was the best vacation ever.

During one of our Sunday afternoon calls, Phil told me he was thinking of buying an old Toyota Land Cruiser for his forthcoming retirement. He couldn't find one in Florida that wasn't rusted but had found one online, in Seattle, and asked me to check it out. I did, and suggested that he come visit, get his truck, and the boys and I would drive halfway across the country with him to tour some of the places our family had seen three decades earlier.

He agreed, and we four Thompson boys drove east to Salt Lake City and down to Zion and Bryce Canyons. We lumbered through Martian rockscapes, twitched down switchbacks through jaw-dropping panoramas. Sean and Leo were serenely quiet for long stretches, tethered to iPods or the iPad loaded with skate videos and *Simpsons* episodes. When one of them grew bored, they'd pick a fight. "Dude stop touching me." "I didn't touch you." "Yes you did." "Shut up." "Quit it." "You quit it." "Ow, dude, that hurts."

My dad turned to me. "Sounds just like you and Jeff."

"You have no idea," I said, wishing Jeff was with us. "That's just their warm-up."

At a remote campsite beside the Colorado River, the boys disappeared to chase lizards as I pitched tents, started a fire, lit lanterns, drank beer, and sipped bourbon with Phil. It grew dark, like a god-switched-off light, and we watched a rising moon set the river ablaze as fish jumped and bats whirled and Art Blakey blew his horn through my cell phone. Our driftwood fire roared. We let the boys drink beer. My dad let them puff his cigar.

"Gross!" Sean yelled, stuffing his mouth with marshmallows to rid the taste. Then Leo grabbed a lantern in the wrong place and we all smelled his burning hand flesh.

The boys and I flew home from Denver, and at the airport I kept texting my dad as he drove toward home—"where u now?"—feeling more melancholy as he rolled away. Each of his replies—"past Amarillo," "east of Dallas"—was a poking reminder that we'd grown briefly closer but were retreating to our respective corners.

Spending eight days on the road with my boys and their grandpa—with Sean and Leo the same age Jeff and I had been—was an attempt to pull my dad close, give him a chance to see the wonderfully wild things his lone grandkids had become. It was the most time I'd spent with Jughead in thirty years.

I felt I'd accomplished something meaningful, though I

couldn't tell what the boys were feeling, after a week apart from their boards. (At one point Leo got a call: "Max? No, I can't skate today. I'm somewhere in Utah.") Yet, just before we'd separated from my dad, somewhere along the final stretch of Colorado highway, Leo had cheerily suggested: "We should do this again sometime. Maybe next summer. Maybe across the whole *country*. Maybe visit skate parks?"

I tucked Leo's idea away, but first we'd have to navigate the transition out of middle school. Thinking back on Jeff and me at that stage, and who we became in high school, brought little comfort. The more my kids reminded me of me and my brother, the more my twitching antennae seemed to be telegraphing something.

I admired the respect skaters showed each other. There was a sweetness to their interactions, all bro-hugs and daps. I loved how they signed off phone conversations with *"Peace."* They were physically close, always high-fiving or fist bumping, punching and shoving, tackling and wrestling. During sleepovers, they'd end the night piled in a heap of sleeping bags, pillows, and blankets, unselfconscious about sleeping side by side with another guy in a single bed, sometimes with feet in each other's faces.

I'd hoped that this pack-of-puppies sensibility would carry on past middle school, that they'd remain some version of sweet and silly, weird and goofy. But lately . . . with hormones kicking in, and high school looming, I'd noticed a shift, a new intensity. One Friday night, I picked four of them up from Inner Space, which they had all to themselves, skating happily and helmetless as if they owned the place. At home, I ordered pizzas then left the boys alone and went out with Mary and friends for drinks.

We came back two hours later and found Nate hobbling around with a huge knot on his ankle and Sean with a bloody nose. They'd been "cage fighting," and Sean was psyched to tell me he'd actually blacked out—"It works! The sleeper hold really works, Dad!" Leo was bummed that he "only saw spots" and had to tap out. In the yard I found pizza boxes, boxing gloves, frayed sleeves they'd scissored off their T-shirts. Inside were bandages, Alka-Seltzer wrappers, open bottles of aspirin. The next morning I found charred cans of butane and WD-40, which they'd tried to set on fire, shards of skateboard they'd shattered with a sledgehammer, and graffiti they'd sprayed in the garage.

They all seemed to be testing out pre–high school personas. Max, normally chill, got into a fistfight with Nate outside Inner Space, which spooked Sean and Leo. And they all practiced gangsta speak. I once heard Leo's half of a phone conversation, which consisted of "What's good, bro? Dope. I'm down. That'd be chill. Hit me up. A'ight. *Peace.*"

Sean and Willem even tried their hand at rapping . . .

> *What am I gonna do with this thug life? /*
> *My weapons of choice are a MAC-10 and a Buck knife /*
> *Too bad, too sad, damn this world is so mad /*
> *What am I gonna do with this thug life?*

The morning after their cage fighting sessions, I eaves-dropped during breakfast as the boys talked primarily about skating and farting.

"It smells because the gas has to go through where you poop," Sean explained. "So there's actually poop particles in it. It's just bad air."

Not thugs, I thought, just *boys*. I was hopeful. Not yet, not yet, not yet, I thought, knowing that a different kind of bad air was destined to soon blow into our lives.

In response to another call of complaint from the manager, I picked up the boys and a friend from Inner Space. Sean and a dreadlocked buddy were both acting silly and cocky, jacked up from the thrill of getting chased by a rent-a-cop.

After dropping off the friend, I asked Sean if he was stoned. He insisted he wasn't—and Leo, brotherly defender, claimed Sean was "just showing off"—but it opened the door to yet another conversation about the approaching storm clouds . . .

"Believe me," I said. "You guys will have plenty of time to experiment later. But *please*—not in middle school."

Sean asked if I'd smoked pot in high school, and I told him sure, I'd smoked some (I didn't get specific), but never really loved it and stopped after high school (mostly true).

"How about coke?" Leo asked.

"Cocaine? *No!*" I said, hoping I hadn't protested too much, not ready to talk about that yet, if ever.

At home, we sat out front in the car, and I told the boys

that I knew, as they knew, that a time was coming soon (if it hadn't arrived already) when someone would hand them not just a joint or a bowl, but a bottle or a pill or some powder, and they'd have to decide—on the spot, right there in front of their peers—*yes or no.*

Leo insisted, seemingly near tears, that they could handle it, that they knew what they were doing. "You can *trust* us," my youngest said.

And I did. I remained hopeful. I scribbled in my journal that night: "I realize they're good kids and I can trust them and we just have to ride out this rough patch."

Of course, it wouldn't take long before both boys would begin saying yes, yes, and *yes.*

Just like my brother and me.

Memories of the day I thought my brother was dead are patchy and imprecise. First there's the shouting out front. Then my parents are running outside. I see a burly dad from down the street carrying something in his arms, trailed by a shrill procession of neighbors.

That something in his arms is Jeff, face covered in blood, his head flopping like a rag doll's. My mother shrieks as they lay Jeff on the lawn to a chorus of *Oh my gods.* I start whimpering, and a pretty Puerto Rican neighbor, Mrs. Bethel, pulls me inside and sits with me and Maura on the scratchy red couch, puts her arms around me and tries to shush me, puts my head on her chest—I'm both terrified and aroused.

I'm not sure how long it took for the information to reach

us, but Jeff wasn't dead, and he wasn't bleeding, he was shit-faced drunk. He and Don's brother, Steve, had helped themselves to a neighbor's Bartles & Jaymes. They'd stumbled around the neighborhood until Jeff passed out on someone's lawn and puked red wine cooler all over himself. Steve panicked and left him there. My parents took Jeff to the hospital, where they pumped his stomach. In my twisted memory of it all, I stayed in Mrs. Bethel's bosomy embrace for hours, her Spanish-accented words soothing and alluring. *"Eets okay now, eets okay . . ."*

Though Jeff notched the first drunken incident of our childhood, I'd soon contribute my own scenes of sloppy stupidity. My brother and I would then tag team through our teenage years, and beyond—just like our old man, who got kicked out of Notre Dame for drinking, something I used to brag about to friends. (He was allowed to return the following semester, and graduated, but I usually left that part out.)

Like many kids of my generation, especially those with some Irish in the mix, I grew up surrounded by booze. Childhood memories are sprinkled with snapshots of Bud cans, jugs of wine, bourbon bottles, pretty cocktails in my parents' monogrammed glasses. I recall smoky parties and the occasional Friday night when my dad would get home from work, plop into his reading chair with a stack of newspapers and a six-pack, where he'd spend an hour or two consuming news and beer. My mom enjoyed her whiskey sours and cheap Chablis.

My high school years had been a constant hunt for beer and weed, and most college nights were spent at parties and bars. As if adding a drunken exclamation point to college, during a postgraduation camping trip with friends we got lost meandering along dark North Jersey back roads until all four of us fell asleep, including the driver, whose fat Oldsmobile slammed into a tree. I was in the front seat, unbuckled, and my face bounced off the windshield, leaving a face-shaped impression. At the hospital, fearful of the police, I declined a doctor's offer to reset my nose, which led to years of sinus problems and, later, multiple surgeries.

As an adult, wine and liquor bottles competed with books for shelf space, and the fridge always had good beer. In North Carolina, when I started writing my book about southern bootleggers, I developed a taste for moonshine's amber progeny, bourbon, and regularly paid Sean's kindergarten teacher to score me jars of real 'shine. If I had to estimate the number of days since college without at least two fingers of bourbon and/or one to two beers? Less than half. Of course, my kids took notice.

When he was younger Sean would staple together sheets of printer paper to create handmade books in which he spun whimsical, unpunctuated, creatively spelled stories. One series featured two crime-fighting pals, Viego and Morgginson, aka Morgi, who loved road trips, treasure hunting, monster fighting, Powerpuff Girls . . . and beer. As they prepared for one of their adventures—pursuing the "abonable snoman and the evil giant"—Morgi began acting strange, speaking in a "completely unintteligent voice," Sean wrote.

Then Viego figured it out: "The reason Morgi that your

acting weird is be-cause you have bin drinking quarts of beer."

Morgi confessed that yes, he had been at Fun Depot, where the waitress "accepted the fact that I wanted beer and that's that."

I wondered . . . What message had drinking beer, wine, or bourbon nearly every night of my kids' lives sent? Had I endorsed an intoxicated household vibe? I always felt I'd been an example of responsible drinking. I rarely got more than tipsy and never spoke in a "completely unintteligent voice." Except for that shameful time I smashed a cocktail glass, I knew my limits. No DUIs. No puking.

Then again, when I complained to a doctor about the recent stress and sleeplessness that came from raising boys—and estimated how much I self-medicated per week (a dozen drinks? *more?*)—he used words like "binge level" and suggested that I ease up a bit. In time I'd realize that teaching Leo to mix martinis hadn't been such a good idea after all. And I'd rightly blame myself for contributing to my kids' coming appreciation for all sorts of substances.

11

On the second-to-last day of eighth grade, just hours before the graduation ceremony—which he was refusing to attend—Sean began making plans to skip school the next day and go skating. It was the annual "Go Skate Day," and his friends were all ditching classes.

I had been working in my basement office and came up to check in with the boys, who were in the kitchen making after-school snacks with three friends, watching YouTube videos, their skate shoes piled in the mudroom atop a sculpture of backpacks and boards. That's when I overheard them talking about Go Skate Day. I googled it and learned that the rogue holiday—scheduled on the summer solstice, the longest day of the year—encouraged skaters to blow off every obligation and just skate. I had to admit, it sounded innocent enough, almost cute.

Then again, hadn't every day been "go skate day" lately?

Sean was telling the others they should warm up at Inner Space first, then hit the streets. But Leo was waffling, thinking about just going to school.

"C'mon, Leo, it's gonna be a good sesh," Sean said, and the other boys hassled Leo until he agreed to join them.

"Wait, wait, *wait* a second," I finally intervened. "Nobody said you could take the day off."

Sean's argument: The school year was done. Middle school was done. Why make a curtain call?

And we were off and running, Sean and I arguing about the value of the next day's classes and of finishing the year with grace. The other boys shuffled outside as Sean and I, like two boxers in a ring, took jabs at each other, a version of the same scuffle we seemed to have all the time.

"Middle school isn't learning," Sean said, in his go-skate defense, and I countered (lamely) with, "But don't you want to say good-bye to your teachers?"

In Sean's case, he'd hardly earned a day off. In recent weeks we'd gotten calls from the vice principal (Sean took a laptop from the library without permission) and the Seattle Police (Sean and friends, skating on private property, taunting the owner, *again*). He'd been having a tough time lately, his grades flirting with the danger zone.

I spent brutal evenings with him, painfully finishing homework that he claimed he'd already turned in, a few of which I found crumpled under his bed. It was as if he'd finished them to prove he could, but saw no upside to giving them to his teacher. But then he hunkered down and did a ton of work to catch up on missing assignments. Mary worked with him, too, and even hired a math tutor. Sean had pulled back from the brink of failure and would be able to graduate on time.

And yet . . . Sean had little interest in graduation. It was difficult to accept how disconnected he was from the whole middle school experience, how we *all* were. Self-inflicted or not, I think Sean felt like an outsider looking in. He'd reached the finish line, but it gave him no sense of accomplishment. He'd done what was needed to close the book on middle school, more than ready to turn the page, even if he might've felt a twinge of regret for not trying harder.

So. When he asked-slash-demanded that I let him skip the last day of eighth grade and go skating . . . let's just say it was a complicated equation.

Late that afternoon, I negotiated a deal: "Go to graduation tonight and *maybe* I'll let you skip school tomorrow."

Hours before the ceremony, Sean finally, somewhat sadly, agreed to put on some nice clothes and attend.

The ceremony was held in the school parking lot on a warm, sunny evening. Students filed into their seats as Mary and I stood off to one side—the sheepish parents who deserved the back row. We'd missed so many middle school rites. No soccer games or class plays, science fairs or spelling bees. My kids wanted to spend as little time as possible at Whitman Middle.

We were relieved to find Sean listed in the program but confused by the asterisk beside his name. During the ceremony, after a few heartbreaking words of remembrance for Joey, the principal described how she would announce each graduate and they'd come to the podium to get their diploma. She explained that students with asterisks by their names were being recognized for academic achievement. I turned to Mary, who looked at the program again to make sure—at one low point we feared he might fail everything except gym.

I was usually the weepy one, but when they called Sean's name Mary started to cry, surprising us both. As Sean bounced up to the platform to grab his diploma I left Mary and sprinted from the back row, just in time to get a photo of my boy striding past his classmates, grinning a toothy grin. He hadn't wanted to be here, and now his friends were whistling and clapping and the sun was shining and he seemed proud and relieved and it just killed me.

After the ceremony, Sean, Nate, Max, and Willem posed for goofy pictures in front of a Whitman Wildcats sign, flashing peace signs and making faces. Mary asked Sean to hold up his embossed certificate (which we'd learn was for high scores on his standardized tests): "to Sean Thompson in recognition of Outstanding Academic Achievement."

That night, I called Willem's and Max's dads and we all agreed (reluctantly) to let the kids skip the final day of school for Go Skate Day. The next morning, a gang of boys came by for breakfast, a blizzard of cereal flakes, jam-smeared toasts, the chugging of OJ. They were so jacked up and cute that I was glad that I'd cut them some slack.

Then Leo changed his mind. He wanted to go to school. Sean was stunned he would choose school over skating. He pleaded with Leo, the two of them suddenly, strangely near tears. Maybe the emotion of actually finishing middle school had caught up to Sean. Caught up with both of them. Or maybe Leo just needed a break.

"I'm not quitting skating, Sean," Leo said. "It's just sometimes I don't *feel* like skating."

Sean finally backed off, slung his backpack and board over his shoulder, and gave Leo a hug.

"Love you, Leo."

"Love you, too, bro."

Later that morning, after Leo walked to school and Sean and his gang went off to skate, I called the vice principal, to catch up and to thank her. I knew she'd been meeting with Sean, trying to find ways to help. Still, he'd been sent to her office so many times I was convinced she must have hated my kid.

Instead, she told me about her daughter, the skateboarder. The one whose boyfriend was a *pro* skater. Turns out she knew exactly what we'd been dealing with, having had similar tussles with her "live in the moment" daughter, as she put it. The vice principal explained that she saw something in Sean, something that needed a nudge.

She could also tell Sean was sensitive and, despite his outward bluster, a little insecure—someone who didn't respond to punishment, but to patience. She described the day Sean skipped a class and came to her office, asking if he could just sit there. She didn't scold him but let him sit quietly, and after a few minutes he asked her about the family pictures on her desk, about her childhood, her parents. When she told him her parents were Japanese immigrants who'd been held in an internment camp during World War II, he asked more questions . . . *How did that happen? What was it like? Could it happen again?*

"That's not a conversation a lot of students would have with me," she told me.

I was stunned. Sean had actually developed a relationship with the *vice principal?*

She said she understood his attraction to the shadowy edge of skating, how the classroom could not compete with the street. In a tone bordering on admiration, she described Sean's wide-ranging curiosity, his sense of right and wrong, his insistent (if sometimes shrill) righteousness. She told me how Sean rarely backed down when he got in trouble, how he'd seek loopholes, boldly challenging the logic of a teacher's rule and repeatedly asking why or why not.

"The thing is?" she said. "He's really a deep thinker. He has the foundation to do great work."

I wasn't sure where this was going . . .

"And these kids who always ask 'why'?" she continued, then paused, maybe afraid to say too much. "The ones who ask 'why?' . . . Well, those are the people who can change the world."

I couldn't speak. My throat cinched tight, and I took a deep breath to keep my cool.

We'd come so far the past few years, with so many authority figures scolding our noncompliant sons for not following the *system*. And the implication was: you're bad parents, doing it all wrong. *Bad!*

Now someone was telling me our son wasn't so worthless after all. In fact, she was suggesting there was hope, that our complicated, recalcitrant, antagonistic, confrontational little man might one day be a force for good. She saw what we saw: the promise (and challenge) of a kid who's been let off his leash, who thinks for himself, who follows his own meandering if imperfect path. Of all things, Sean's middle school vice principal was the therapist I didn't know I needed.

As we talked I jotted notes on Sean's pre-high school summer reading list, scribbling in the gaps between Kurt Vonnegut, Ian McEwan, Jhumpa Lahiri, Dave Eggers, Tom Wolfe, Sherman Alexie, Zadie Smith, Salman Rushdie— writers who'd been *my* teachers during my own periods of asking why and why not.

I thanked the vice principal for her help, hung up, and mixed a huge Manhattan.

While waiting for Mary and the boys to get home, I started highlighting names on the reading list—Cormac McCarthy, Donna Tartt, Tobias Wolff, David Shields— and quickly found myself crying, tears dribbling onto the marked-up reading list. I'd always been an easy crier, a trait inherited from my mom, my eyes leaking on cue for sappy TV commercials, corny songs, heartfelt movie scenes. Today's tears felt justified and earned. We'd reached some culmination of the things I'd tried to tell myself—my kids are unique and challenging boundary pushers with so much potential and all I can do is love them, believe in them, give them room, wait and hope and pray. And sometimes drink.

We'd heard all those typical bad-boy diagnoses over the years, all those acronyms, even if the doctors, therapists, teachers, and counselors never seemed quite sure. Even Sean at times wanted to know: "What's wrong with me? What do they *call* it?" He wanted a name. We'd received many. But none of them fit.

Now we had another name. One that made more sense. He was a boy who asked why. A *lot*.

Mary finally got home and joined me with a cocktail and I started telling her about the vice principal, but I had to keep pausing, struggling to get the words out, trying to keep my composure, but failing. "She told me . . ." I tried again, but couldn't speak without sobbing. "She said kids like Sean . . . that they ask *why* . . . that they change the . . ."

Before I could choke out "change the world," Mary knew. She started to tear up, too. I put my face in my hands and I let go, a boozy, weepy fucking mess.

As I often did at times of parenting drama, I desperately wished I could've shared Sean's graduation saga with my mom. But I also realized that she would've surely reminded me of my own inglorious departure from middle school. And she would've added some snark, like "apple doesn't fall far from the tree, does it, NT?"

In the sunny final days of eighth grade, I'm sitting in the back of Mrs. Beihl's class, my mind already on summer— late '70s, AM radio, hostages in Iran, bad hair—when the spell is broken by my mom's appearance at the door, her face crimped in a scowl. She gives the urgent "come here *now*" finger curl and I walk out of class, toward my comeuppance.

Minutes later, we're at the Sparta Police Department, in the office of Sergeant Irons. On his desk is a check made out to Sparta Sporting Goods for $65. In the notes section of the lower left, in my own black-ink scrawl, "Happy Birthday Neal." Printed in the top left corner is the name and address of a neighbor, i.e., not my parents. And Irons is *pissed*.

"Is that your handwriting there, Mister Thompson?" the officer asks, and I'm already shaking my head *no*.

The check had come from a classmate's house, though I can't recall whether Don and I stole the checkbook while hanging there after school or, worse, if we broke in later. I do remember Don and I each tearing out a few checks and Don's brother holding on to the rest. I'd used one of my checks months earlier to buy a ski sweater, telling my curious mom that Don had given it to me because it didn't fit him anymore.

"Don't you dare lie to me, young man," Irons said, raising his voice to scary-cop level.

I turned to my mom for help, but she kept looking down

at her hands, seething and ashamed. Irons slammed his fist on his metal desk and barked, "Mom's not gonna help you out of this, son. You need to tell the truth." On the car ride home, after I'd tearfully confessed, my mom looked so disappointed and hurt: "What the hell's wrong with you? That's *not* how you were raised."

That night, despite my pleading, my dad drove me to the neighbor's house, and on their front stoop I stammered an apology. They agreed not to press charges.

I still look back on that day as my adolescent dumb-ass wake-up call. Or one of them. Sergeant Irons didn't quite scare me straight, though. There was more idiocy to come.

Maybe that's why Sean's middle school completion, while a relief, also left me a bit uneasy. Would things settle down in high school? Having put my parents through the wringer in high school, I knew the answer. And it scared the crap out of me.

So. With Sean soon to start high school, and Leo entering his last year of middle school, I felt a ticking-clock urgency to spend more time with them, cling to them, be a better dad. That's when I remembered Leo's idea from the previous summer as we were driving through Utah with my dad.

And I planned a road trip.

INTERLUDE
SK8 THE ST8S

Wiping out is an underappreciated skill.

—Laird Hamilton

CLEVELAND, OHIO
SUMMER OF 2011

Five teen boys and two grown men, squished into a huge SUV, hemmed in by skateboards, video gear, sweat-skanked clothes. Doritos bags, soda cans, and water bottles at their feet. A record-breaking heat wave simmering outside, the air-conditioner groaning. Seven of us, lost in Cleveland, and I'm wondering why I thought this was a good idea.

Sean pokes our iPad screen, zooms in and out on a digital map, desperate to find a skate spot he'd seen on YouTube. Using the Google Maps satellite view, he searches for a little plaza surrounded by housing projects. "We're close, we're close!" he yells, unsure, close to panic. *Pinch and zoom*, treasure hunting for a patch of Cleveland concrete.

We've been on the road for five days and our adventure is imploding. We should be sprawled out in a converted 1972 school bus, but the bus died in South Carolina before rolling a foot. "The last thing we need right now is getting lost in a Cleveland slum," I say, eager to keep pushing toward Detroit. I want to support Sean, but I have that nagging feeling I'd had in New Orleans five years earlier, driving through the Lower Ninth researching a post-Katrina book—I feel like a ghetto tourist.

"We'll be back on the road in thirty minutes," Sean says, then scolds: "and it's hardly a *slum*, Dad."

I appreciate my sons' curiosity about the off-piste corners of the world, which YouTube and their online skate community have helped shrink. They've come of age at a time when a

Seattle kid in the back of a Ford Explorer can find an inner-Cleveland skate spot with an iPad. I'm cool with that. But we're behind schedule. And our stinky SUV is due back to Budget Rental at St. Louis airport in three days. Unless we find replacement wheels we'll be stuck halfway into our cross-country skate park tour.

Still . . . one reason we're on this fathers-and-sons trek is to experience a nontouristy, mostly urban version of America, including the concrete jungles that have become my kids' playgrounds. So I grudgingly pulled off I-77 and follow my fourteen-year-old's spotty instructions. "Don't worry," says Sean. "We're really close. I *think*."

After a few laps around a neighborhood that could be a stand-in for Baltimore in *The Wire*, Sean yells, "Turn here!" A few hundred yards later we're in an alley, and Sean checks his on-screen satellite view and yells "stop!" He jumps out, turns down an alley, and with a glance back at the SUV is gone. My first thought: Mary's going to be so pissed.

Sean finally emerges from the alley and skips back, wide-eyed and giddy. "We're *here!*" The other boys grab their boards, and my pal Lou and I swap nervous looks as all five boys—his son, my two, and their two friends—skate past the NO GUNS! signs toward a plaza of concrete ledges, banks, and a trapezoid-shaped platform topped by a Japanese-looking sculpture. I'm thinking: We risked our lives for *this?* Sean, as if hearing my thoughts, yells: "I'm not scared . . . Maybe I'm a little scared."

The boys roll across the plaza and begin ripping ollies and kickflips, rock-to-fakies, and board slides. Another skater arrives, then another, and the plaza is transformed into an impromptu skate park. A young girl walks by tugging twin boys, five or six years old, in matching cargo shorts and Gap T-shirts, and Leo rolls up and offers his board: "Wanna try?"

The twins' eyes light up and they look to the girl, who shrugs. Our crew starts giving skate lessons, holding the twins' hands, towing or pushing them. One kid juts out his arms and strikes a surfer's pose, "Check me out!" It's cute, but I'm thinking: What if he falls and cracks his skull?

Later, as we head toward Detroit, Leo's buddy Nathan writes our daily blog post, summing up the Cleveland detour: "Most parents wouldn't have done that."

And I'm not sure if I should feel proud or ashamed.

The idea had started small, but word spread quickly, and we soon had an entourage.

Sean and Leo would each bring a friend: Willem for Sean, Nathan for Leo. Three dads latched on: my decades-long friend Lou, with his son Niall, who'd known my kids since babyhood; Reid, Sean's elementary school teacher from back in Asheville, who'd become a good friend and now lived in Charleston; and Willem's dad, Paul, an old-school skater who'd join us for the final few days.

When I launched a Kickstarter campaign to raise money for an RV or van—calling our project "Sk8 the St8s: a coast-to-coast, fathers-and-sons adventure"—friends gave me shit for taking their money to pay for a vacation. But I'd convinced myself their investment was serving a greater purpose. With the boys teetering on the edge of a new school phase, and me on the verge of an upcoming career transition, I wanted to take a few weeks to immerse myself in the sport and culture that had come to dominate our family lifestyle.

"This is no vacation," I told friends and reluctant donors. "It's a *mission*."

Our mission was to drive a giant S across America, from South Carolina to Oregon, where I'd drop three of the five boys at a weeklong skate camp outside Portland. Along the way we planned to interview skaters and skate dads, chronicling the skate scenes of Middle America on a blog and on YouTube. A former high school classmate who worked for CBS saw our Kickstarter campaign on Facebook and offered to help with the blog and have CBS radio stations interview the boys in a few cities.

The $4,500 we raised was supposed to pay for a 1979 school bus nicknamed Bustaride, owned by a friend of Reid's. Air-conditioned and wired for sound, with a lava lamp and shag rugs, it was a dorm room on wheels. The boys couldn't wait to flop into one of the beat-up couches.

"That bus is gonna smell like ass cheese in a few days," Reid teases as he drives us through Charleston toward our pre-planned rendezvous with the bus.

That's when we see Bustaride's hood propped open like the maw of an giant alligator, three men standing on the bumper, staring into the engine well.

Bustaride is busted.

Reid and I plunge into Apollo 13–style contingency mode, ditching nonessentials at his house, the minigrill, camp gear, food, my guitar. In his wife's SUV, which we dub "Trusta-ride," Reid drives us to Richmond to meet Lou and his wife, who shuttle us to their home outside D.C. Reid says he'll re-join us in Los Angeles, "If you ever get there."

After a flurry of calls to RV and car rental places, all I can find is a seven-passenger SUV at Reagan National Airport, which I'll have to return in St. Louis four days later. "I'll take it!" I yell, putting our adventure back onto a wobbly track.

The next day's USA Today carries a full-page, color-coded map showing most of the country locked in a record heat wave. The red zone? We'll be rolling straight through it.

I'd hoped that spending three weeks on the road with my sons would unravel the mysteries of the board. I'd crack the code. The Matrix would be revealed. And I'd become a better dad. But now, without the bus, and without Reid as codriver and third adult, I'll have to scale back my roles as interviewer, videographer, and ethnographer and step up as driver, naviga-tor, and a few other unanticipated roles. And instead of camp-ing and sleeping on the bus, we'll need lots of hotel rooms.

After our Cleveland housing project detour, a biblical deluge seeps through our not-so-waterproof rooftop carrier. So when we check into a two-room suite in Detroit—scored via Hotwire . . . "the nicest hotel room I've ever stayed in," says Nathan; "Me too," I add—we drape the entire suite with rain-soaked clothes.

The boys explore the hotel and I flee to the bar, order a bour-bon and a beer, catch up on blog posts and e-mails to RV renters. When Lou walks in I have no time to hide *either* of my drinks and feel like I've been busted by my parents. When we'd met twenty-plus years earlier, Lou had hair to his ass, played shirtless guitar in a killer college band, smoked and drank prodigiously. Now, he's a father of two, a government employee, a lung cancer survivor, and sober—or, as he puts it, "retired."

He'd signed on to the road trip in hopes of sampling a taste of his old life—"It'll help me reconnect with my inner punk next door," he'd said. Instead: our kids are the punks, and we're the babysitters. "Um, our *gentlemen* are fucking around in the weight room," he says, not commenting on my two-fisted drinking.

I drink up, close my laptop, and find the boys shirtless and pumping weight machines beneath "adult supervision" warning signs. Something about their heedless fun and my uptight obligations tweaks me, and I light into them like some dickwad gym teacher.

"You guys are supposed to be helping," I whine, then turn to Leo, who'd promised to make a skate video for our blog. "I need *help*, here!"

The boys dive into heaping mounds of red-sauced pasta, buttery bread, and glistening salad greens, our first home-cooked meal since D.C. We're in Chicago, at Mary's aunt Gerry's house, where our scuzzy clothes twirl in the washer as we tell Gerry and Uncle Ed about the trip so far. I sit off to the side, keeping the video camera rolling, capturing the tense mood . . .

Niall: "I don't like the situation with the car. It's a little too small for me. But I love skating all the spots."

Lou (with a quick glance toward me): "You know what? I think we're better off when we just let them . . . *skate.* That's what they're here to do, right? And we're here to just, like, buy water and drive them around and get them Skittles."

Nathan: "I dunno, I've just had so much fun so far. I mean, I don't even know what day it is. It doesn't even matter anymore. It's gotten to a point where I don't even care. It's like, I'm with my friends, doing something I enjoy more than anything. I love it, actually. I dunno, I've had the greatest time so far."

After dinner, Uncle Ed takes the boys to Wilson Skate Park beside Lake Michigan while I stay home with Gerry and do laundry.

When the boys return, Leo pulls me aside. He's getting mad that I keep working on the blog and videos instead of being part of the trip.

"I wish we'd never agreed to the stupid blog," he says. "I just want you to have fun and you're not having *fun.*"

Thankfully, a beer from Ed and a Xanax from Gerry helps me slide into a floppy sleep atop a blow-up mattress on their floor.

After a brief skate session beneath the silvery St. Louis arch, eyes alert for cops while illegally parked beside the Mississippi River, the boys (and Google Maps, and our iPad) lead us west into an industrial underbelly. Beneath Kingshighway Bridge lurks a homemade park built by skaters from cast-off materials—chunks of sidewalk mortar, slabs of marble countertop, metal oil barrels, concrete highway barriers, jagged sections of swimming pool, blue-tiled NO DIVING letters still visible.

"Oh, this place is *sick*," says Willem, who throws himself into the park like a toddler plunging into a playground. The others follow, weaving between bridge abutments, rolling up molded waves of concrete, ollie-ing over trash cans and coils of garden hose.

Littered with trash and abandoned furniture, hemmed in by a storage warehouse and a vacant parking lot, cars and trucks rumbling overhead, Kingshighway Bridge is a place for drug deals and prostitution, for dumping carpet-wrapped bodies. And just right for skating. Sean dubs it "full-on guerrilla."

I'll later google it and find the *St. Louis Post-Dispatch* description: a *haven for a counterculture group of nonconformists*.

Watching them lost in a fugue state of blissful skating, I borrow Leo's board and try rolling around, though I've clearly lost every bit of skill I once had as a preteen skater.

Then, reluctantly, I call it—"Time to go, boys . . ."

Having had no luck with vehicle rentals, I've been desperately browsing Craigslist for something to buy. Mary's sister, Katherine, has e-mailed about a few possibilities, including a fifteen-passenger church van near their home in Columbia, Missouri. Cheaper than an RV rental, the "Jesus wheels," as she called it, could keep our trip alive.

I drive to a Bank of America and withdraw $3,500, then return our armpit-smelling SUV at the St. Louis airport. Lugging our gear through the terminal, I keep patting my ass to make sure the cash is still there. During the two-hour shuttle ride to Columbia, we all silently mull our prospects: if the Jesus wheels doesn't work out, we'll be stranded.

That night the boys watch a horror movie as I stand in my sister-in-law's kitchen, slurping a beer, then another. I stood in the same spot (also drinking) three years earlier, halfway into our family's cross-country move from North Carolina to Seattle, with me bringing up the rear as Mary and the boys got settled in our new northwest home.

Tonight, Katherine and her husband, David, join me in the kitchen and Katherine asks the obvious, "Bite off more than you can chew?"

I know she means the road trip, not everything else—the move to another new city, the boys and their skating, my stalled writing career, our family's roller-coaster life . . .

I also know the answer—road trip, boys, skating, career, life—would be the same.

"Maybe so," I say, and finish my beer.

In a parking lot in Jefferson City, Missouri, Pastor Mike holds out his hand and I resist the urge to hug him.

Mike tells me his fifteen-passenger Dodge had been used for years to transport prisoners to and from the county jail, where he works as chaplain. He'd bought it for church outings, and the words GRACE FAMILY WORSHIP CENTER are still faintly visible beneath a recent coat of white paint.

"What a blessing you are to those young people," Mike says when I describe our road trip. I tell him *he's* the blessing, then offer him an envelope of $100 bills and thank him for saving our trip. I drive off, listening to country music radio, grinning like a goof and trying not to cry with relief as Willie Nelson, as if the pastor had conjured it, warbles (no lie), "On the road again . . ." The AC fucking *cranks*.

Back in Columbia, the boys dive inside, stroking the five rows of vinyl seats—one row per skater—as if they're Corinthian leather.

For our inaugural drive, Katherine and David lead us to a swimming quarry. As I dive into the cool water, the ogre that's been thumping inside my chest calms to a dull ache, and I allow myself to believe, for the first time in a week: maybe we'll make it to Portland after all. But we still have a thousand miles to go.

In the new prison-cum-church-cum-skate van, we detour into Joplin, Missouri. It's been two months since tornadoes maimed this town, and at first the boys just want food—"Let's go to Chili's"—but then we see the mounds of rubble, the wiped-clean house foundations, a car on the roof of a half-smashed school.

Nathan wonders where everyone is sleeping, and Niall marvels at the random pattern of destruction, one side of the street ravaged, the other side intact—"like gerrymandering," he says, and Lou and I exchange raised eyebrows. *Gerrymandering?*

It feels a bit ghoulish, but I can't help myself, the journalist in me guiding us along the path of devastation, past neighborhoods swiped into oblivion, past an RV with a banner advertising TRAUMA COUNSELING & PRAYER. All around are the ragged remnants of domestic life—lawn chairs and a busted Santa statue, carpets and clothes, toys and TVs.

After a few "holy shit" comments, the van becomes hushed. I feel my throat clench and look over at Lou, whose eyes are as misty as mine. I hear sniffling from the back, and wonder if this was a mistake. Niall and Leo share blogging duties that afternoon, and Leo writes: "We have never seen anything like Joplin. It was like a horror movie. All of us were scared to be there. We all got teared-up looking at this town . . . We couldn't believe the devastation."

Niall writes: "I saw places where once there was a happy neighborhood, where people were having potlucks and parties that now looked like the prairie."

South to Tulsa, then Plano, then Dallas, where we score another Hotwire deal at the swanky Fairmont. The boys play a game of commando through the halls, earning the wrath of the security team as I escape to the lounge, order a Woodford on ice, start blogging and planning, missing the fun. Though I'd toyed with the idea of not drinking at all on the road—in solidarity with Lou, and because I knew it couldn't hurt—that idea got flushed after Bustaride died.

Comfortably buzzed, I rally the crew for dinner, detouring along the way to another place of tragedy, Dealey Plaza. A tour guide helpfully shows the boys the book depository window and the grassy knoll. The boys read the plaques and tourist brochures. As we walk on toward Sonny Bryan's Smokehouse, I hear them talking . . . politics?

"There were such high hopes," says Sean, the 2012 election more than a year off.

"There still are," Willem says. "But he hasn't done everything he said he would."

The other kids nod as Lou and I share double takes.

"Don't get me wrong, Obama's great," Willem continues. "But you can't fix everything in one presidency."

Driving through the shimmering 112-degree heat of West Texas into New Mexico, Lou and I take turns on the iPod, dragging each other back to the nostalgic core of our musical prime, the '80s. The Replacements give way to Elvis Costello, the Cure, Haircut 100, the Smiths, both of us swinging our arms, playing air drums and air guitar.

Then Lou dials up some Turkish surf music just as the western sky darkens and sparks with lightning. "Are those tornadoes?" one of the boys asks.

The trancelike monotony of the westward haul toward L.A. becomes a trippy highlight—more boredom, less panic.

With the boys sitting peacefully in their rows, with Google Maps to guide us, coffee in the cup holder and tunes on the stereo, I feel in charge and in control. The landscape reminds me of Buzz Aldrin's description of the moon: "magnificent desolation." The boys keep themselves surprisingly content, whiling away the hours with less screen time than I expected and few "how much longer" complaints.

I wonder if all that hanging around skate parks developed a comfort with the in-between moments. They seem so content, so patient. I only regret I didn't plant an audio recorder in the back of the van, to capture their far-ranging conversations about skating, school, friends, girls, farts, food, sharts, Snooki, *Jersey Shore*, and more politics.

"I'm voting for Nader," Nathan says.

"Watch, he'll get elected someday and he'll be the best president ever," Leo adds.

Sometimes I look back and see them all lined up, listening to music or not, staring out the window or straight ahead, and I think: Did I get this right?

A ten-hour drive from Dallas ends with the boys skating the chutes of a concrete arroyo beneath a Motel 6 sign outside Albuquerque. The next day, en route to Tempe, Lou pulls out a camera to "interview" Niall, Sean, and Willem about their upcoming entry into high school, which awaits on the other side of our trip like a foot-tapping schoolmarm.

"I don't wanna be really rich and kinda sad," Niall says. "I'd rather be, like, middle-class—with a family and a job that I can go to and know I'll be happy."

"I don't want to be too ambitious and try to do something like skateboarding or become an artist of some sort," Sean says. "Because it's very difficult to make money or be a success doing that."

That one stings a bit. Is that how Sean views me, "an artist of some sort"? He's surely witnessed the "difficult to make money" part.

Willem says he wants to be an architect, but Sean, who's almost as hard on Willem as he is on Leo, cuts him off.

"Willem . . . architects *design* buildings. Maybe you can be a construction worker."

Willem just grins, but Sean keeps going: "You see, me and Niall, we're like Macs. We've got taste, style, and a strong Internet connection. Willem? You're kinda like a Dell."

I tell Willem to go ahead and punch Sean, but Willem keeps on silently grinning.

"Hold on," Sean says. "He's still loading."

What we eat: chips, cheesesteaks, scores of peanut butter sandwiches. During one lunch stop we realize we'd lost our plastic knives so Lou scoops out peanut butter with his fingers and smears it on white bread. A successful meal to me is Subway—at least they might get a little lettuce. Success to us all is our first In-N-Out burger fest.

What we drink: Gatorade, energy drinks, an occasional

soda, gallons of coffee. During a Starbucks stop everyone orders frothy mocha drinks except Willem, who asks for milk. "Make it a venti," he says, which the others find hilarious.

Even funnier: the In-N-Out next to the Kum & Go.

We also drink many gallons of water from scores of plastic bottles bought by the case. The scrunchy bottles become playthings, noisemakers, weapons, and, maybe inevitably, piss receptacles. At one rest stop I discover a collection of yellow-filled bottles stashed beneath the seats. Thankfully none sprung a leak.

During a roadside pee break we venture off the highway onto a dirt road into a spooky patch of Arizona desert. We find a dried-out elk carcass and hunt for rattlesnakes. We decide to cover up the faded WORSHIP CENTER on the van with all the stickers we've collected from skate shops, turning the process into a time-lapse video for YouTube.

That evening I leave the boys and Lou at the Tempe skate park to buy a case of water and sandwiches for dinner, then linger at a strip mall coffee shop for an hour. When I get back I stand there watching Lou on a bench watching his son skate beneath gauzy lights. It reminds me of all those hours I'd spent on the fringe of a skate park as my kids did the thing that made them happiest. It hits me: *this* is what the road trip is supposed to be all about. Not seeing America, just skating—for five hours straight.

When I ask Lou about it later, he says he became mesmerized watching the boys in their zone, and had an epiphany of his own.

"They had the freedom to do nothing but skate," he says.

"No school, no rebelliousness. Their minds were clear. They were unshackled by any constraints. They were intense and determined, but serene and calm. They skated like it was their fucking *job*."

In Los Angeles, skateboarding's birthplace, we hit a dozen parks and spots. We watch pros flying and grinding and spinning at Hollenbeck Park and Stoner Plaza. The boys ollie on and off picnic benches at YouTube-famous Lockwood Elementary, and security guards kick us out of Santa Monica High.

And then . . . we lose Sean.

Reid has flown to L.A. to rejoin the road trip. He starts the afternoon at a rooftop bar and texts me "join me at the hotel erwin?" Lou agrees to stay with the boys at Venice Beach Skatepark while I escape to meet Reid for a cocktail.

I find Reid at the railing, Jim Beam in one hand, smoke in the other, talking to a tall, multiply pierced guy called Seven. I order a bourbon and bum a cigarette off Seven. After two weeks in the company of five teens and my alcohol-free copilot, a drink and a smoke with grown-ups is just what I need. We look down at a drum circle on the beach, out toward the setting sun exploding behind Santa Monica Pier, and just as I reach near euphoric relaxation Lou calls: "Have you see Sean? We can't find Sean."

I stub out my smoke and race back through the freaky heart of Venice, past tattoo parlors and a procession of chanting Hare Krishnas, to look for my son. When I get to the skate park, Sean still hasn't rejoined the others. (First thought:

Mary will *kill* me.) After a few worrisome minutes, I get a text from Reid: "sean is here with me."

Sean had somehow overheard which bar I was headed for, googled the place, walked away from Lou and the others, then talked his way up to the rooftop and found Reid. I sprint back to the bar and take pictures of Sean and his ex-kindergarten teacher, high above Venice, with a dude named Seven photobombing behind them.

One of the first to visit Sean in the hospital after his accident, Reid now tells his ex-student: "Never would've guessed then that we'd be at a rooftop bar together in L.A."

The next day, Lou and I part ways with a kiss-on-the-lips farewell that's become our hello/good-bye over the years. He and Niall are headed home to D.C. while the rest of us are bound for San Francisco.

"Thanks for taking me outside my comfort zone," Lou says. "I needed that."

"Likewise," I tell him, and wrap him in a bear hug.

Is it true, though? Have I fully tested my discomfort? I'm so grateful to Lou for adding a gnarly new chapter to the story of our twenty-year friendship, and I'll remember certain moments—Cleveland, Pastor Mike, Joplin, West Texas air guitar, dead elk, Tempe—forever. But I worry I've been too much of a bitchy babysitter: "buckle up!" "brush your teeth!" "charge your phone!" Also, being around my sober friend only highlighted how frequently I sneak off for a glass of something to tame my stress.

Yet, in his final blog post, penned from D.C., Lou essentially reminds me to stop worrying and just enjoy the ride . . .

"That's the most fun I've had in a long time," he writes. "I hope I was an able copilot, or yin to your yang, or sumpin'. I love you man."

A t Portland's Amtrak station, the midday train arrives from Seattle and out steps my beautiful wife, who clutches our boys and bursts into tears as I wrap myself around them all. Our family has never been apart for so long. Everyone piles into our van and we drive to a hotel, where Mary and her sons huddle and catch up. Tomorrow, we'll deliver three of the guys to their summer skate camp. But tonight? I'm finally off duty. Of course . . . I crave a drink. And Reid is there to oblige.

"Do y'all have minibars?" Reid asks the Crown Plaza concierge.

"No, sir."

"How about a megabar?"

He and I rush off like naughty boys, find the hotel lounge, and order a bourbon and a beer apiece.

As a skate-obsessed teenager, Reid had pinched his dad's VW Beetle to drive, with no license, to a Bones Brigade skate show an hour from his home. He's now a college professor, a red-bearded surfer with a wife and daughter. He's been part of this trip all along, rescuing us from early disaster, following the blog, commenting on Facebook. Now, having joined us from L.A. up the coast, with four drinks in front of us, he wants details, hungry for assurance that it's been a success.

We talk for two hours—about skating, drinking, God, boys, the South, and the origins of my kids' defiance, which Reid had glimpsed as Sean's teacher. It's the longest I've been separated from the boys in three weeks. Eventually, Reid asks, "Did you find what you were looking for?"

Across five thousand miles and nineteen states, we visited two dozen skate parks, some famous and iconic skate spots. My kids added twelve new states to their life list, and had now skated nearly half of them. We met scores of skaters, pros, kids, dads, skate shop owners, and not an asshole in the bunch. But did I find what I was *looking* for? I suppose I'd secretly hoped for an *a-ha!* revelation, for some wise old skater to pull me aside and explain it all, like Morpheus in *The Matrix*.

I tell Reid about a few skate sessions—through New Mexico arroyos, beneath a St. Louis bridge, in a Cleveland housing project, at skater-built FDR skate park beneath I-95 in South Philly, where a CBS Radio reporter interviewed the boys, all wearing their "Sk8 the St8s" T-shirts, asking them, "So what do you guys really like about skating?"

They all took turns trying to put it into words—"it's kind of hard to explain," Sean said—until sweaty-faced Willem thought for a moment, stroked his fuzzy chin, and said, "For me? Skating is a way to express my creativity. It's kind of like an art form." Nathan popped Willem a wide-eyed look like he'd just spoken Klingon.

"I'm not sure *what* I was looking for," I tell Reid. "I was in survival mode for three weeks."

I'd at least learned that my kids' art form was best accompanied by a whiff of danger, the risk of assault or arrest. At their "guerrilla" spots, the boys found their zone. They were focused and fearless. No expectations, no pressures, no teachers or parents. It all sloughed away in those wildcat destinations. Maybe that's what this trip has been all about, delivering a few memorably off-piste moments.

My boys and their friends seemed happiest out of bounds.

It wouldn't click until years later how much the road trip reflected our family life, and how much I still had to learn about that. In one of my "Sk8 the St8s" notebooks I'd later find scribbled clues to my future self . . . *freedom of the road, detours off the beaten track, improvisational, rash, messy, harried . . . wild ride, unpredictable, best plans get trashed . . .*

And I'll laugh when I later read this, apropos of the road trip and so much more: *need to pivot and adapt, be patient, try to enjoy the moments of peace and beauty.*

Reid finally asks, "Did *you* at least have some fun?"

I flash back a few days to a session at Third and Army in San Francisco, where Sean kept encouraging me to try an ollie. I'd grabbed his board, right foot forward, pushed with my left, rolled ten feet, pushed again, made a few wobbly kick turns, tried to hop, but failed. Sean just rolled his eyes. "Are you trying to look uncomfortable?"

After all those miles and all those skate parks, I'd traveled less than a hundred yards on a board.

I confess to Reid: "Man, I think I forgot how to *skate*."

PART 3
SMOKING AND TAGGING

sually I felt a murky mix of pride, guilt, and defensiveness when I told people I wrote for a living. Curious and/or dubious, they'd ask, "What do you, like, *write?*" I'd explain that I wrote nonfiction books and magazine articles. "And you get *paid* to do that?" To some, it sounded like I played video games or scrapbooked for a living.

Lately, my writing had indeed begun to feel more speculative, like panning for gold each day. My first book was published in 2004, followed by two more over the next three years, but the third book sold poorly, a trajectory interrupter, like being sent back three spaces. I wasn't a household name or a bestseller. I'd been scrambling to finish my Robert Ripley biography and racing to find a new project, my up-and-down income trending downward. I began fretting that I was letting my family down, that I'd deluded myself into believing my passion for storytelling would pay all the bills.

So. On the fourth anniversary of my mother's death, I dug out an oversize suit jacket and drove to downtown Seattle for a day of back-to-back interviews at Amazon.com. Before the road trip, I had applied for a job as an editor on Amazon's books team, where I'd curate best-of lists, review books, interview authors, write stories for a books blog. It seemed like an author's dream gig—and, given the slowdown in my writing income, after a decade of self-employment, a timely lifeline.

I doubted that Amazon would hire a writer who worked in his basement, but I felt I had to give it a shot. Afterward, exhausted from so much adult-human contact, I bought a six-pack and a bottle of Dickel, bags of candy for the boys, then sat drinking in the backyard, taking photos of Sean and Leo skating, waiting for Mary to get home, and wondering . . . *What the hell did I just do? What if they actually want to hire me? Who'll be here for the boys? Who'll chauffeur them to skate parks?* Fears of getting pulled back into the mainstream workforce and losing a connection with my kids had contributed to the inspiration for the road trip, but now it was over, and my skate dad days were truly ending.

When Amazon offered me the job, just a week before the road trip, Leo wanted to know all the details. What are the perks? Do I get Amazon discounts? What's my office like? I found it impressive and unnerving that he wanted to know the financials—How much would I make? What's the retirement plan? I think the real question was, *Is this going to take us up a notch?* "I'm excited about your new job," he said, adding (wisely) that it'd be good for me to get out of the basement and meet people. "I'm excited *for* you!"

Sean was excited that I'd be working at a new corporate campus whose plazas he'd skated during construction, the scene of numerous security guard confrontations. I wanted to be psyched, too, but as the moment neared, I felt conflicted. Did accepting a corporate job make me a quitter? Or a realist? Was I turning my back on everything I'd tried to build over the past ten years? Or was I kidding myself down there in the basement? Mainly I worried: Had my experiment as a creator failed? Would I ever *write* again?

Mary, who had been ridiculously patient and supportive during my years of writing, was as thrilled as Leo, in a way that made me worry that a day job was overdue.

I'd once read a news story about Seattle's new breed of seed investors, VC funders, incubators, and told Mary, "They should have angel investors for writers."

"They already do," she said. "They're called wives."

With our income stabilized, Mary and I decided it was time to find a real home, and our weekend neighborhood walks became epic house-hunting ventures.

Eight months after starting my new job, we made a lowball "short sale" offer to an owner who'd overborrowed. It had been four years since our move to Seattle, years that coincided with the collapse of the housing market. The hoops we had to jump through with banks and mortgage companies were like a combination obstacle course and minefield. Our closing kept getting postponed, then we ran into delays selling our property back in North Carolina. For months, Mary and I were crabby and snippy with each other. My workdays would end with the weak hope of a jog or a yoga class but usually led to a drink or two, and a tense wait for the boys to come home from skating.

I was convinced that a new home—in a nicer part of town, with a bedroom for each boy, and a large family room to replace the leaky concrete-floor basement—would solve a bunch of problems, give the boys a secure base as they tried to figure out how to be teenagers and high schoolers. A new home would ground us all, I was sure of it.

While waiting for the sale to go through, Leo graduated from eighth grade and Sean wrapped up a bumpy freshman year of high school. Then, like coils that had been squeezed by the daily expectations of classes, homework, and curfews, the boys sprung loose that summer. It was the first summer in years that neither Mary nor I were available to drive them to day camps, skate parks, or on mini road trips. Which left them mostly unrooted and free, with their bus passes and plenty of time to skate and seek trouble.

Sean: Sitting on a park bench near his high school, eating a sandwich as a friend walks by. The friend pulls out a pipe, offers Sean a hit. The cop parked nearby in an unmarked car watches Sean take a deep drag, then swoops in as the other kid runs. Sean reluctantly gives the cop his name, initiating a case that will drag on for more than a year, beginning with the letter we receive stating, "The prosecutor's office has reviewed this offense report and found it to be sufficient to file a criminal charge..."

Leo: I call to see when he's coming home and... "Heyyy, dad-man! How are youuuu?" He's *bombed*. He got separated from Sean and the others and isn't sure where he is. I tell him to stay put and I call Sean, who tells me where he last saw Leo. I drive there and eventually find Leo stumbling down a dark sidewalk alone. I lead him to the car, buckle him in, then he gurgles, "Uh-oh." I get him unbuckled and onto the grass just in time. We repeat the dance—buckle, "uh-oh," unbuckle, *hurl*—two more times.

Sean and Leo: The two of them come home skunky and grinning, so blatant about it, as if they'd sealed themselves in a smoke-filled closet. Which they had: smoking inside a fast-food joint's tiny restroom after worming their way into Seattle's annual cannabis celebration, Hempfest.

Though we'd had a couple minor smoking incidents during middle school, seemingly overnight the smell of weed now began to accompany our family dinners. If we wanted a conflict-free meal, Mary and I would have to pretend Spicoli wasn't at the table, snickering at us all. We tried to convince ourselves that with both boys, now fourteen and fifteen, set to attend the same high school come fall—followed soon after by our tenuously scheduled move into a new house—that they'd settle down. We *all* would.

Then again, looking back on me and my brother at that same precarious, midteens, early-high-school transition stage... well, that brought little comfort.

One of my finer high school moments: skipping class in the girls' locker room with Janey, sipping from a plastic bottle of *jungle juice*—gin, whiskey, tequila, vermouth, schnapps, and some green shit called Midori, siphoned off from my parents' liquor cabinet. I show up late to class, pick up a fire extinguisher, and pretend to aim it at my friend Blaise. Suddenly a stream of fire retardant is spewing from the nozzle, foaming against the blackboard. I can't shut it off, so I drop the canister and try to run, but Father Daley shows up, grabs me by my plaid Catholic school tie, chews me out while dragging me to the office to face Father McHugh.

Daley and McHugh had come to our parish straight from Ireland, young, funny, and charming. When I was six or seven, McHugh came to our house for a first communion party, and I remember him laughing with my Irish nana, the two of them sloshing back glasses of red wine. Now he was my high school principal, and I was the drunk one, and he wasn't laughing. In his office I apologized, as McHugh dialed my mom and asked her to come pick up her drunk son.

Weeks later, McHugh saw me in the hallway, late for class, and asked, "Mr. Thompson, shouldn't you be in fourth period right now?"

"*Relax*, Father," I said, followed by other poorly chosen words, and suddenly found myself shoved up against the lockers by a red-faced man of the cloth.

"That's *it*, mister," McHugh barked, then stepped back and swung a thumb-pointed arm like a ref ejecting a baseball player. "You're *outta here*."

My expulsion was thankfully temporary. After an Irish

mafia–type consultation with my mom, McHugh agreed to reduce my punishment to a weeklong suspension.

During my suspension, I hitchhiked to a friend's house, carrying a bong I'd made from a Popeye shampoo bottle. On the stoned hitchhike back home, the male driver said he'd take me all the way to my house if I let him blow me. I told him to stop, to drop me right there beside the highway, but he kept driving and smirking. "No, stop, *now*," I yelled, opening my door and preparing to jump until he all-too-slowly pulled over. With the car still rolling I leaped, tumbled into the grass, and ran to a nearby bar, where I called my mom from a pay phone. While waiting, I reluctantly tossed the Popeye bong into the bushes.

My beleaguered mom usually had a "knock it off, knucklehead" attitude toward these and other antics, but even she was getting fed up.

"Better get it together, mister," she said on the drive home.

And my dad? The way I remember it, he mostly just seemed so *disappointed* in me. Too many nights I'd be waiting for him to get home to inflict punishment—a scolding, a grounding, the threat of a belt-whooping. Many years later he told me his worst arguments with my mom were over controlling and corralling me and Jeff during high school.

"I always had to be the bad guy," he recalled, then added: "But maybe we weren't firm enough . . ."

The summer before my sophomore year of high school—a year after my check-forging incident—our family moved out to the country. Some may find it hard to imagine New Jersey "country," but this was the real deal, nowhere near a turnpike exit. We lived across from a defunct mink farm, more cows and sheep than humans as neighbors. Our house, a mossy A-frame, sat atop a wooded hill, reached by a switch-backed dirt driveway. My top-of-the-"A" bedroom had western views of hills crawling with tractors and combines and the state's highest hills beyond that. It felt off the grid, boreal, remote. We were North Jersey hillbillies—*Jersey-billies?* I think my dad wanted more breathing space.

Jeff and I complained about leaving behind our friends at our little beach-and-boat community, and I wondered what I'd do without my skateboards and water skis out in farmville. But our parents, rarely indulgent, offered a remarkable bribe: a motorcycle. Jeff reminded me that they actually gave us a choice: keep a boat on the lake, or get a dirt bike. We chose the latter, and my dad drove us to the seller that my mom had found in the want ads.

At first, we were supposed to ride our battered Hodaka Ace Super Rat only up and down the driveway. Of course, we were soon tearing down the street, across the jagged turf of the ex-mink farm, racing through pastures, exploring dairy farms and railroad beds. My dad would chew us out if he caught us riding in the street, but we pushed him and my mom, pushed our boundaries, inch by inch, day after day, ditching the helmets and venturing way out of bounds and wearing our poor parents down.

The Hodaka was the first in a series of motorcycles. Eventually Jeff and I each got our own, and one day I flipped mine and landed upside down on my helmetless head. Another day I gave a friend a ride and we veered off the road, flew up and over a stone wall, and landed in a tangled heap as Jeff looked on in terror. My friend—son of a local dentist—lost a tooth, and I twisted and scorched my ankle on the muffler. In time I began to slow things down a little, but Jeff sped up.

Jeff's favorite bike was a frighteningly fast Yamaha MX 100, and I'll always remember it as the vehicle that contributed to our divergence.

Convinced that the Catholic school wasn't equipped to address my brother's disinterest in school—and his dyslexia, which would go undiagnosed for way too long—my mom transferred Jeff to the public high school. I kept commuting back to our old town to attend the Catholic school, while Jeff made a new set of countrified motorcycle-riding friends. At our isolated new home, I skated less and water-skied less while Jeff thrived on his two-wheeled machine, his version of my boys' four-wheeled boards.

At his new school, Jeff hung out with kids who could milk cows, fix cars, wield a hammer. Against our parents' wishes, he got a dog—and, against school rules, brought his dog to class. Until that time, I'd reigned as the family fuckup. But Jeff, waiting on deck, would surpass me, a rapid escalation in motorcycle wrecks and alcohol-fueled antics.

Like the time he stole some kid's dirt bike, T-boned a car at fifty miles an hour, flew over the hood, tore a chunk out of his thigh, and almost bled to death while running from the cops. And the time at the Action Park amusement park built at our local ski area, when he decided to climb hand over hand along a chairlift cable, from his chair to the one behind his. But Jeff's timing was off, and just before losing his hands to the pulley wheels he let go and dropped forty feet, shattering both ankles and wrists.

When I went off to college in Pennsylvania, Jeff drank a few Bud "nips" one morning—the same eight-ouncers my mom's mom used to drink—borrowed the car I'd left at home (my dad's old Datsun 510), and on the way to school rounded a curve driving way too fast, suddenly in the path of an oncoming truck. He swerved off the road and flipped the car, bouncing it end over end into a field, barely missing a few trees and landing on its roof. He crawled out of the wreckage, miraculously unhurt.

For some reason, I kept a framed picture of that squashed orange Datsun for years. I think it reminded me that Jeff had grown more impressively, if dangerously, adventurous while I, with each passing year, played it safer and became more cautious.

Jeff and I inherited a mix of influences from our parents; Jeff got more Jughead genes, and I got more from our mom. My dad loved motorcycles, guns, sports cars, boats, airplanes— his "toys," my mom called them. My mom, who grew up poor in a New Jersey housing project, collected paperback novels, cookbooks, and thrift store clothes as her toys. My dad's included a BMW motorcycle, then a Suzuki, a wooden sailboat, VW bugs, a Lotus, the army ambulance, and an International Harvester tractor, which Jeff and I drove up and down the driveway and once almost flipped. After I'd left for college my dad started taking flying lessons, bought an airplane, and later started building a kit plane from scratch.

While my mom was happy to escape into a novel—a trait she passed on to me—my dad loved being on the road, on the water, in the air. Like Jeff, he loved speed and freedom, loved to *soar*. Well into his seventies, Jughead continued to ride a motorcycle (a Harley), drive a ragtop Mini Cooper, scuba dive, and fly his kit airplane.

For work, I read an E. L. Doctorow novel in which he described surfing, skiing, and other outdoor hobbies as "free rides of the planet . . . there for you to get on or get off or get killed." My father and brother sought those free rides. They feared less. And what worried me: What if Leo and Sean were genetically predisposed to seek the rides that could kill them?

At a family wedding, in response to my griping about our risk-taking skate kids and their budding fondness for bud and Bud, my brother's wife laughed, pointed at my brother, then at me, then at my dad—each of us with drinks in hand—and nearly shouted . . .

"What did you *expect?*"

13

Mary and I were a good (if erratic) team. Across eighteen years of marriage we took small but (for us) life-affirming domestic risks. We bought, remodeled, and sold houses, hopped from town to town, changed jobs and careers, not content or able to stay put or sink roots. Before we married, Mary got laid off from a job in finance and made a major career pivot to start over in the film industry, as a freelancer. In my midthirties, with a wife and two young kids, I'd quit my newspaper job to write books. The boys had seen me and Mary work for ourselves since they were toddlers. We both apparently thrived on the chaos that came with empowered independence.

During my years as a stay-at-home writer, I'd sometimes think back on my dad's stabs at self-employment, including the engineering company he started (called, interestingly, *Innerspace*) and a stint selling real estate. Similarly, Jeff had long been his own boss, running his own construction company, his own plowing company. Were all of us allergic to teams and rules and hierarchy? Resistant to being *managed*?

Then there was Mary's dad, who'd been a dentist with his own practice, who'd invested in real estate, whose success had allowed him to retire in his early fifties—another "lone wolf" in the gene pool, as Mary put it. "The men in our families? Obedience is not in their vocabulary," she once said, though we both knew she spoke the same language.

Yet we balanced each other out. If one of us threatened to veer too far—"Let's move to Ireland!"—the other (usually Mary) reined it in: "Whoa! Um, *no*." Then again, "balance" sometimes meant pendulous shifts in our family mood. Mary was hopeful and optimistic. She really *wanted* to believe some of the boys' stories—like the homemade water-bottle bong we found behind the recycling bins, and Leo's response: "Maybe a neighbor put it there?"—while my first assumption was usually "bullshit!" I was a cynic, a skeptic, an Irish-blooded screamer, quick to anger and quick to tears. I wrestled with sleeplessness, anxiety, financial stresses, and booze.

It's not like we were street buskers or carnies, but in our own ways Mary and I—as kids, and now as adults—had been persistent challengers of convention, endorsers of rule bending, pursuers of a life in motion. Lately, though, it felt like we were beginning to reap what we'd sown, paying tithes to the Church of Independence. At a work retreat, when asked to share something personal, Mary told the group: "I'm stressed-out all the time because I've got *two . . . rebellious . . . boys* at home." And the others nodded in sympathy.

By seeking freedom in our lives, had we sent a message to our kids that they deserved it, too? The same message our dads had conveyed to us?

Then again, we sometimes caught a whiff of some discomfort with the lifestyle they'd been born into. One night at the kitchen table (before I'd started working for Amazon), Sean had grilled Mary with a series of unexpected questions: "Are we doing okay? Can we pay our rent? Are we saving for college? How much money do you guys make?"

The main question that dogs every married couple is: *Are we going to make it?* For work I once interviewed the author Andre Dubus III, who described a period when he and his wife, after twenty-five years of marriage, watched friends' relationships crumble. They'd cling to each other at night, as if on a life raft—"We're okay, aren't we, honey?"

That's why, when we finally moved into our new life raft of a Seattle home, just before Christmas, Mary and I simultaneously sighed a giant *aaaahhh.* . . .

With Leo a freshman, and Sean a sophomore, we now craved stability, a solid home base for the boys' high school years. I was so relieved to have finally rooted us. I was a 9-to-5-er. I wore a company badge, clipped to my front pocket. I'd become a semilegit grown-up. Though I continued to write in the mornings and whenever I could find an hour or two (and would publish my Robert Ripley biography the next summer), I was a late-bloomed corporate employee, with a 401k and, optimistically, a small college fund.

I still felt occasional stabs of sadness that I was no longer the guy I'd wanted to be since childhood—full-time author—but I'd grown comfortable with and even proud of the new lifestyle. It felt adventurous in a new way, and necessary. Because the plan for the next few years was: one house, one school, no drama.

A few nights after moving in, Mary and I gave friends a tour of the house, a 1920s bungalow on a small lot, a half mile from Puget Sound. Our mismatched furniture and eclectic tchotchkes seemed to have found the right vessel. Mary's mom's oil paintings, my jars of moonshine, Mary's Led Zeppelin action figures, the framed pictures of the boys skating, toddler-era ceramic sculptures beside a creepy clown carving and all those books—my books, friends' books, books by authors I'd interviewed and admired—it all kinda worked.

We then walked to a nearby Italian restaurant, and over cocktails and calamari someone inevitably asked, "How are the boys?" Our friends' kids were excellent students in private schools, all girls, so the question was always a tricky one to address. Sometimes I'd feint: "Fine, good. How 'bout your kids?" Sometimes I'd come clean, sheepishly describing some skating-related incident. Other times I'd attempt to cover up my embarrassment with a "boys will be boys" story, which was the tack I took tonight.

While walking to the restaurant, as if scripted for maximum shame, Nate's father had called to tell me about spying on Nate and Sean as they tried to roll a joint in his backyard the night before. Instead of breaking up the scene, he watched them fumble with the rolling paper and meager nuggets of pot. They passed around a lumpy spliff that began to fall apart before they could smoke it down. "I mean, *I* could've rolled a better joint," Clark said, laughing and almost relieved that they appeared to be amateurs.

I told our dinner mates about it, and they obligingly chuckled. Our friends were kind, reassuring. "They're good kids," one of them said.

It's something I'd heard from other friends and family: "They're good kids. Don't worry. They'll be fine." I truly believed they were *good*. I wanted to believe they'd be *fine*.

That night in bed, Mary and I awoke to the overpowering smell of pot curling up from the basement family room. Two floors below our bedroom, that room would all too quickly become their playroom, their hiding place, their late night smoke shack.

One Sunday afternoon I was in the basement watching football when Sean came down carrying a case of Coke.

He clearly wasn't expecting me to be there, and he seemed nervous.

"Where'd you get that?" I asked, pointing to the Coke, which he hugged tightly to his chest.

"Oh, um, Max's dad gave it to us," he said. But instead of putting it in the basement fridge, he took it to his room.

We rarely drank soda in our house. The boys didn't like it, and neither did Mary and I. A case of Coke made no sense.

The next day I found the box tucked beside the furnace,

a towel stuffed into the opening. Inside was a sculpted, rainbow-colored glass bong that could've passed for a Chihuly flower vase. My first instinct was to smash it. But honestly, it seemed too pretty. As I mulled over the appropriate parental response—confront Sean, throw it out, ignore it, smoke it—I started looking around the family room, wondering what else might be hidden. It didn't take long. In a cabinet I found a plastic spice jar, repurposed for a different kind of herb.

It killed me that they'd decorated the jar (formerly labeled MARJORAM) with a "Sk8 the St8s" sticker.

More than a year past our fathers-and-sons road trip, I'd clearly misread some of the terms and conditions of the evolving skate life.

I walked past our back door at the exact right/wrong moment to see Sean reach beneath the back porch to stash something.

"What's that?" I asked, stepping outside to catch him in the act.

Pause. Stare. Showdown . . .

"Well, what do you *think?*" he finally said.

"Drugs?"

"Why do you have to call it drugs?" he asked, using air quotes.

"Well, what is it?"

"It's just *pot.*"

Washington State voters didn't help our cause.

In late 2012, we joined Colorado as the nation's kush-friendliest state. Initiative 502 would enact all sorts of concessions to cannabis, to be phased in over the coming year. It was as if my friends and neighbors had conspired to decriminalize, say, arson. I felt betrayed, and pissed. While I was happy to have both boys in the same school, less than a mile from our home, it was there—the school I'd soon picture as an open-air pot market with optional academics—that my kids' skater lifestyle took a sharp turn into Stonerville.

The legalization momentum coincided with a new phase in our house, the start of a cat-and-mouse game that would dominate our high school experience.

Incriminating evidence practically fell into my lap. In a sock drawer my hand bumps something hard: a glass pipe rolled inside two pairs of socks. Skimming through Leo's Christmas camera: shots of a hoodied skate friend puffing on a blunt in the front seat of someone's car. Same camera: a glass pipe balanced atop a weed-filled spice jar beside a lighter, displayed on our kitchen counter. Stuffed under Sean's bed: the nylon camera bag I'd been looking for, soiled by flakes of herb and crumpled rolling papers.

"But pot is *legal*," the boys would say, when confronted with the evidence.

"Not yet it's not, and not for *you*," I'd counter, reminding them of the details: like booze, pot would be legal for adults, but not teenage boys.

They'd roll their eyes. *Whatever,* Dad.

They began leaving the basement windows open, the whiff of voter-endorsed smoke lingering. I drafted a "Rules of the House" list, the first of which was: "No drugs or drug paraphernalia in the house." They both hated the *D* word. In their minds, pot was a plant not a drug.

The other rules were an attempt to set benchmarks for grades ("anything less than a C is unacceptable"), attendance ("don't skip class and don't be late"), curfews, chores, and jobs ("find one, keep it, take it seriously"). But really . . . all the rules tied back to rule number one. Violations were punishable by groundings designed to hurt them where it mattered most, by keeping them off their boards. Despite their indignant howls, I made them sign the document.

When I told a writer friend how my teens had suddenly become pot devotees—a bag of Lays "Baked!" potato chips displayed on Sean's bookshelf, a poster of Bob Marley in midtoke on Leo's wall—she laughed . . .

"*Oh* . . . I like your kids already," she said.

But what did her reaction really mean? Why did my fellow Gen Xers have such fond memories of their own teen stoner years? Was it nostalgia for marijuana's simpler DIY days? I mean, the only paraphernalia my friends and I ever possessed was rolling papers and *maybe* a pipe. The rest was all homemade—shampoo-bottle bongs or makeshift bowls made of a pin-holed beer can or a gouged-out apple and some aluminum foil. But now? Pot had gone high-tech and high concept, and the good stuff was ten times stronger than the shit I smoked in the '80s. Legalization had created a fetishization for get-stoned devices, a validation of the smoke-and-skate lifestyle.

All of which made enforcing our house rules a constant battle of feints and half-truths.

Looking for schoolwork in Sean's backpack one afternoon I found a silver grinder (for shredding buds into easy-to-roll shreds), a tamper (for packing bowls), a fancy butane lighter, rolling papers, and a package of Phillies Blunts. It confirmed my escalating suspicions that he was no longer an amateur. Further confirmation: the cardboard toilet paper tubes we started finding in the basement, stuffed with dryer sheets—homemade filtration systems, to collect their exhaled plumes.

I placed the evidence from Sean's backpack on the kitchen table, and waited.

When he got home and gave me a hug, I sniffed audibly, then stood back and held out my hands in a WTF pose. He reeked like Bob Marley.

"I was *skating*," Sean said.

As in: what did you *expect?*

t started small, just a few thumb-size tags penned in car-toony bubble font on textbooks and skate decks, practice versions in notebooks and on printer paper. As they tested different styles and colors we'd find the words *Acres* and *Aztec* on the back of shopping lists, homework assignments, in the margins of our *Seattle Times* and *New York Times*. Then they began experimenting with domestic defacement, using black Sharpies to inscribe their desks, dressers, closet doors, and other bedroom surfaces.

"Acres" was Leo's tag, sometimes written "Acre$," named for our Happy Acres home back in North Carolina—a reflection of Leo's pride in his funky, hillbilly past. Sean's tag (which has been changed here to "Aztec") was born of a school report he wrote on ancient Mexican culture, a portion of which extolled the virtues of one particular tribe known for being major stoners, toking Jimson weed, ingesting peyote or 'shrooms.

Acres and Aztec. Freedom and fun. Bounty and bliss. I doubt my kids assigned much symbolism to their tags. But that's how I viewed them, as reflections of their respective mojos. In time, these two words bloomed across surfaces like a fungus, hundreds of Acres and Aztec tags crawling along bedroom walls and furniture. In the absence of other art-making endeavors, I actually didn't mind the domestic tagging and probably implicitly endorsed it. As a former teen wall painter, I recognized the intent, if not the art.

And it seemed harmless enough, to let them decorate their own rooms, just as I had. As Mary and I often did, we rationalized: Maybe they'll become artists? They did take a few art classes, pottery and drawing, though anytime we encouraged a deeper exploration—art history, or maybe join Seattle's public art program—they'd roll their eyes and explain with disdain that they cared about graffiti, not street art and certainly not *art*-art. Graffiti was something to be lived, not learned in a classroom.

On the lookout for common ground, I'd snap pictures of graffiti and text it to the boys. I'd bring home books from work, on Banksy and street art, and once tried to get them to watch a TED talk by a French graffiti artist, but they scoffed, as if I'd suggested a family math test.

I'd also clip rap and hip-hop reviews from newspapers and magazines until Leo told me: "I don't listen to the kind of music they write about in the *New York Times*, Dad."

During a Friday night happy hour with Mary, I found myself whining—about the graffiti infestation, the ever-present pot smells, the bass-heavy music that thrummed up from our basement, all that foul-mouthed stoner rap: Action Bronson, Andre Nickatina, Riff Raff, Chief Keef. Mary stopped my rant and scolded, "You really hate them, don't you?"

She was kind of teasing, but her point: I was becoming harder on them. Which I suppose was a cliché. Like dads across time, I'd begun to seriously question my sons' musical taste, their style of dress, their commitment to school, their sanity. And instead of compartmentalizing—I'm glad you're doing *this*, but I wish you'd do less of *that*—I started lumping my complaints together: the mediocre grades, the skipped classes, the stupid weed, the out-of-bounds skating, the rip-a-bong rap, the late nights, and now the graffiti.

But my message lacked nuance. If I criticized one piece—*stop smoking!*—it was as if I was criticizing their entire way of life. I was becoming a "bad dog!" machine—the bad cop that my dad feared he'd been at that stage—always reminding my kids of their shortcomings. The effect was a downer, for me, for Mary, for them.

Me: "If you keep making bad decisions, it becomes a habit, and suddenly your decisions all suck and—"

Sean, interrupting: "Yeah, I know, and then I'll be homeless."

Me: "Worse than that. You'll be *unhappy*."

Leo: "Dad, when you talk to us like this it makes me feel like you don't *like* us."

Me, indignant: "I . . . I *love* you guys! *And* I like you. But I can't pretend I like what you're doing."

I could feel my critiques and admonishments making them sad (Sean) or angry (Leo), but I seemed incapable of finding the right language, of putting a positive spin on things (like Mary), of encouraging and inspiring like a good coach, unable to hide my disappointment and my worry. I felt a distance growing between us. And it scared me.

One weekend, after one of my Friday night, please-don't-smoke arguments—"It's your kryptonite!"—Leo dialed up some drama . . .

"I'm sorry, okay? I'm sorry I'm a disappointment. I'm sorry I'm sorry I'm *sorry*. This is who I am! And I know what I'm doing. Nothing you say or do is going to change that."

Later that night, he texted: "Sorry for overreacting." And an hour after that, the words I craved: "I love you!"

I texted back: "You're hardly a disappointment." Then: "But my job is to help you be your best—and pot does not help with that."

No reply.

My father and I weren't close during my teen years. And probably for similar reasons: bad son/disappointed dad. In our new house in the country, I lived far from my school friends. I had my motorcycle and still occasionally hitchhiked, but I wasn't driving yet and spent lots of time at home. Sometimes I'd watch old movies with Maura, or one of her favorites, like *The Boy Who Could Fly*. Often I'd hike in the woods or hang in my room alone, playing guitar and writing shitty songs, bad poetry, and short stories. I smoked some pot. Hash, too. Not much. Usually just a pinch burned through a homemade bowl or minibong.

Unlike the search-and-destroy missions I waged on my kids' rooms, my parents gave me plenty of space. I doubt they smelled me smoking—I was cautious, not blatant. Or maybe they didn't feel the need to spy. Or maybe they just didn't care. Also, I'm sure my jazz-listening dad (WBGO Newark) was happy to avoid the music I blasted in my room— Allman Brothers, Lynyrd Skynyrd, the Clash, the Who, Neil Young, Genesis, and, primarily, the Grateful Dead— especially when the album-themed wall paintings began.

At the tip of our A-frame, my bedroom ceiling pinched in on me. I'd get a little stoned and paint music-themed murals, covering the angled walls with oil-painted album covers: the Dead (*American Beauty, Blues for Allah, Europe '72*), the Who (*Tommy*), even Journey (*Captured*).

When I later asked my dad about that, he remembered "some character, probably from the rock world. I think he was dressed in a zoot suit . . ." That would've been the dancing dude from the back of *Shakedown Street*, which I'd modified by replacing his snapping fingers with a fuck-you gesture, which Phil made me repaint.

A full third of a century past the events of my high school

days, Phil and I finally talked by phone one Sunday afternoon about my pot smoking and Jeff's (thankfully temporary) fondness for cocaine. My father observed: "I worried mostly about drinking, not dope. In retrospect, I guess we did give you too much space. I was pretty naive."

Walking home from a Ballard bus stop one afternoon, while crossing an intersection I looked up to see the red-white-and-blue oval logo of a "Sk8 the St8s" sticker that someone had slapped onto the post of a street sign. It made me smile, thinking back on that wacky road trip two years earlier.

I took an iPhone pic and kept walking. A hundred yards later, another one, atop a yellow fire hydrant. Another picture. Two blocks later, one more sticker, covering up the NO on a NO PARKING sign. I texted the photos to Mary—"Sk8 the St8s trifecta!"

Had they been there all along, and I'd just walked by? Or were the boys still carrying stickers around, looking for places to leave their mark? In time, I'd find "Sk8 the Sk8s" stickers on bus stop benches, stop signs, mailboxes, and bike racks. I once looked up to see one right in front of me on the back of a bus seat.

Those stickers reminded me of how hopeful I'd been before our road trip, but how little I'd actually learned since. Like not seeing graffiti in our future.

Stickering, it turned out, was just a warm-up, an introduction to public defacement. Though I'd hoped that it would stay in the basement, our weird family secret, their tagging moved out into the open. As it was always meant to, I suppose.

While walking the dog one evening past the Nordic Heritage Museum I spotted a football-size "Aztec" spray-painted onto a garage bin. Beneath that, a sideways "Acre$." I stood there for a minute, seething as Mickey tugged on the leash. I was relieved they'd at least picked a discreet spot on a dumpster. At the time, I told myself: at least their law breaking wasn't *too* blatant. Later, I told them both: "Knock it off!"

Then came the stages of escalation. They'd come home with paint-spattered hands and shoes. I'd find spray cans in their backpacks. While running or walking the dog, I scanned neighborhood surfaces, looking for evidence on playground equipment or park benches.

Perhaps inevitably, I received a call one day from the Seattle Police Department's Graffiti Unit. My first thought: a unit just for graffiti?

The officer said Sean had been spotted spraying graffiti on a utility shed beside some railroad tracks. Someone had followed Sean home, called the cops, gave them our address. An officer eventually came to the house and talked to Sean, who admitted to the deed, even though he and Leo frequently insisted that graffiti wasn't a crime. Like street skating, they viewed it as a public expression of their creativity and freedom.

The Seattle Police Department disagreed.

The officer explained to me by phone that graffiti was a gateway crime, and he suggested we keep a close eye on our boys. "They're looking for attention," he told me, poking right at my soft spot, stoking my fear that we were headed down a dark path—whose trailhead I'd led us to.

One night, walking Mickey around that same Nordic Museum, past the now-painted-over Aztec and Acres tags, I saw three hooded figures near the playground, standing beneath ribbons of smoke. Mickey began tugging, and as we approached the cloud-enshrouded trio I realized it was Sean, Leo, and Willem, each pinching his own joint. In my day, I kvetched in my head, joints were for sharing, not one apiece. As I neared the boys I threw Mickey's leash at Leo and left, pissed and incapable of saying a useful word.

Truth is: they weren't causing trouble. They were teen boys sharing tokes. Three joints was more than I'd have liked but still not that different from what I'd done at their age.

"Oh, I like your kids," my writer friend would have said.

"You hate them," my wife might've said.

But . . . which was it? I loved them desperately. But as Leo hinted: Did I *love* them but not *like* them?

Or was it the pot I really hated? In high school, I'd appreciated the three-beer, two-hit buzz but never craved the white-noise drone that came from getting fully baked. And after college I came to actively dislike being stoned, the aroma evoking a confluence of emotions—I hate you, I miss you. Age tweaked my tolerance. The last time I'd gotten truly stoned had been a decade earlier, back in North Carolina on assignment for *Outside* magazine, fly-fishing in the Great Smoky Mountains. Reid had joined me, and two hits off his pipe turned me full-on zombie. Everything shut down. I couldn't speak. As David Carr once described it: "like driving through life with the parking brake on."

I couldn't understand why my *sons* would want to feel so dopey all the time. I was also miffed by the unwillingness to hide it, the gleefully defiant in-your-*face*-ness of it. If I never saw any of it, I wonder if things might've been different. But I'd find shit tucked behind Harry Potter books, in the Sonics lunch box, in the cartoon-covered minisuitcase Sean got as a toddler, in the glass jars we gave them as piggy banks one Christmas. Under their beds, in the attic, in the workshop, under the front porch. My house rules had become a house joke. I'd toss shit out, battle the "you stole my stuff" accusations, but the weed and its assorted delivery systems always came back.

"Like weeds," Mary once quipped.

Then I crossed a line and began snooping on their phones. In the mornings while they slept, I'd unlock their iPhones with the four-digit PINs I'd swiped, and find photos of dime bags, bowls, and blunts. I'd read suspicious-sounding texts from names I didn't recognize. I once sneakily mentioned one of those names to Sean.

"How do you know that name?" he asked.

"Saw it on your screen—a missed call," I lied. Then: "Who is he, your dealer?"

Sean looked like he wanted to play dumb, but his anger got the best of him, and he yelled, "He's just a kid I buy pot from!"

And Leo, becoming more argumentative and lawyerly by the day, would regularly accuse me of exaggerating, hyperbolizing, and cynically assuming the worst. He would challenge me: "Do you really think we're out there getting drunk and stoned all day every day?" (Um, *yeah*.) "Cuz we're *not*. We're just hanging with our friends!"

I had no way of knowing the truth, but he was right that I imagined pot as an accompaniment to everything they did.

During after-work drinks with a few colleagues one of them asked about my kids. I wanted to say "They're great." And probably should have. Instead, I played the woe-is-me dad thing, which I should have been sharing with a therapist: "They're experimenting a lot these days . . . with herb." A coworker accurately pointed out that anytime I talked about my kids, usually the second thing out of my mouth was *pot*. Had it become my obsession? Had fixating on my kids' pot-smoking hobby become *my* hobby?

With Sean asleep on the couch, I grabbed his phone, hacked in, scrolled through his texts, piecing together the night's fun. Then I went into his room, sniffing and snooping like a bloodhound. Neatly arranged inside the Sonics lunchbox I found a glass bowl, rolling papers, shredder, tamper, matches, lighter, and two little bags of moss-green weed—a veritable pot-smoker's fun kit. "Shit, shit, *SHIT*," I yelled, as Sean slept on and Mickey ran and hid.

I wanted to drag him off the couch, scream at him, spank

him. Instead, I laid it all out on our dining-room table and took drug-bust photos. Late the next morning, when he awoke and saw what I'd found, Sean started his indignant "violating my privacy" argument, but I cut him off, reminding him of the Rules of the House.

Sean said if I kept stalking and harassing him he'd end up like his friend who always whined "I *hate* my dad."

"Is that what you want?" he asked. "You've changed lately, man . . . You're not the same."

I never imagined feeling worse as a dad than I did after Sean's accident. I never thought parenting could get harder than waiting for CT scans to make sure my boy didn't have brain damage on top of a shattered leg. At the time, I'd prayed, "Please, Lord, get him through this—just keep my son *alive*." In darker moments, I'd wonder if I was doomed to pay a price for that deal. I also wondered if Sean's very survival was a source of my fatherly incompetence. Since he didn't die, had I overcompensated in letting him just *live?* After all, this was a kid who thought he saw God, who'd developed a singular tenet for himself: "Why did God give us lives? To have *fun*."

"Sean, listen . . . each choice you make, each decision, it all adds up," I said, knowing that years of lecturing and yelling rarely made a dent. But I felt desperate to wrest back some control, to regain some authority as the *dad*, so I kept going . . . "And when you string together a bunch of bad decisions? Pretty soon you're headed down a *bad* road."

"But, Dad, it's *my* road. *My* life," he said. "Why can't you just leave me alone and let me live my own life?"

"You call this living?" I said. "Staying out all night and sleeping all day?"

"I'm a teenager! Ninety-nine percent of teenagers sleep until noon . . . Smart kids. Kids who'll grow up to be millionaires."

I felt the conversation slipping away.

What he wanted from me was acceptance: of the pot smoking, the graffiti, all of it. He wanted me to let him be the person he wanted to be.

"I know what I'm doing, Fudge-luff—even when it's wrong," he said, then summed up the biggest parental challenge of all: "You have to *trust* me."

Sean later texted an apology: "Sorry about this morning. I was grumpy and tired. I love you. But you have to trust me."

At dinner, I grabbed him in a bear hug, squeezed him, buried his face in my neck. Mary and Leo cleaned the table as Sean and I walked out back to talk. He said he was worried that I put too much pressure on myself, wished I could just relax, be happier, or at least less mad. He hated seeing me beat myself up for things my sons were doing or not doing.

"That should be on *me*, not *you*," he said.

Late that night, I found a note in my bedside drawer. He'd typed and printed it that morning, after our fight. It was a full page long, single spaced, longer than most of his school essays. Some of it was woeful (and sadly accurate)— "you are never satisfied with anything I do"—but the lines that brought me to tears came at the end . . .

I have been in a very sad/angry state lately and I think it's time for us to stop butting heads and for you to trust me and my intelligence to get me through life safely. Just relax and don't worry . . . I'm going to find a niche eventually and my life will be fine. I got things under control. I love you dad.

15

The sound of skate wheels on rough pavement—a rattle-chatter like rocks and billiard balls tumbling inside a bingo cage—always triggered my sprint to the window. After moving into our new house, my boys developed an infuriating habit of skating down the driveway into the street. With a cursory car check, they'd turn right, then left, propelling themselves with their push-off foot down 65th Street. My ears became attuned to that sound, like a dog waiting to bark at the mailman. I'd rush to the nearest window and watch them surfing east toward the bus stop, bound for a friend or a skate park or a party. I once saw Leo texting as cars whizzed past; I once watched Sean fire up a cigarette. I'd beg them to skate on the sidewalk or at least do a better job looking for traffic. They'd insist that their finely tuned spatial awareness told them when cars were near.

A decade after Sean's accident, I could still hear the screech of those Toyota tires, that driver's screams, and always would. So anytime I heard the sound of boys skating into the street, I'd brace myself for screeching and screaming. It finally happened one day when I heard Leo skate the driveway then heard squealing tires and ran to the window. Instead of an accident scene I saw Leo's little blond head in the backseat of an electric-blue muscle car, the driver burning rubber as he fled.

Great. We'd entered the phase where my kids' friends were driving, which meant my kids were passengers. One more thing to fret.

When our friend Lorraine was in high school, she and four classmates left a house party, but the driver was so drunk Lorraine refused to get into the car. She tried to convince the others to walk with her, but they just razzed her and drove off. On the walk home, she heard the impact and soon reached the wrecked car, wrapped around a tree. "I should have stayed with you," one friend whispered just before she died beside the road.

That story haunted me. It occupied head space beside two drunk-driving deaths during my high school years, another during college, plus my brother's multiple nonfatal hospitalizations. I would remind Sean and Leo about Lorraine's friends and Jeff's incidents as we entered the "oh shit" stage of parenthood, during which sixteen-year-old *kids* started getting permits and licenses and driving muscle cars.

I reminded them again after one of their friends drove drunk into the ass of a parked car, and another stole his parents' car and flipped it. Those accidents—fortunately with no injuries—launched a series of scary near misses as we descended into the murkier mucks of high school.

Like the time Willem got hit by a garbage truck.

He was skating down a sidewalk, wearing earbuds and a smile, on his way to meet Max for a ride to school. Sitting in his dad's car, Max had a perfectly terrifying view as Willem ollied off the curb and into the street, made a smooth left-hand turn with his back to oncoming traffic. Whatever music Willem was listening to drowned out the sound of the truck's blasting horn and screeching brakes. The truck's front grille punched Willem in the backpack, like a bully's shove, and sent him flattened onto the pavement, facedown, centered between the truck's tires, which squealed to a stop on either side of him. The terrified driver pulled Willem out, shaken, bruised, scraped, but okay.

Weeks later, Sean called me in an agitated state, talking fast and frantic.

"Dad, don't worry, we're safe, it's okay, the police are here," he said. "But I almost just got *killed*."

Sean and a friend had been out skating and were sitting at a bus stop when a car veered off the road and straight at them. They had no time to move. At the last possible second the car twitched right and hit a tree—a small one, which bent over their heads but didn't break. The car stopped just ten feet from where the two boys sat, staring right at the drunken old man behind the wheel. I left work to pick them up and was floored at their good luck. Sean was right: if not for the skinny tree, they might've died.

Suddenly it seemed to me, mischief and danger lurked everywhere. Cars, trucks, graffiti, cops, booze, drugs. I once read author Dennis Lehane's take on fatherhood fears, which reflected my own: "I don't see electrical cords anymore; I see electrocution." Back in North Carolina, sledding with the boys in a park, Mary and I had watched helplessly as Leo and his saucer sled veered off the main sledding path and crashed into a tree trunk. That's how things felt now: instead of a safe path forward, I saw tree trunks.

A sport and a lifestyle and a group of comrades that I'd mostly supported now seemed like a dangerously volatile mix. Innocent fears about my kids not wearing helmets or not crossing at a crosswalk were replaced by terrors that clenched in my chest and haunted my daily thoughts. Fear enshrouded me. I put it on each morning like bad cologne.

More than anything I dreaded that middle-of-the-night phone call, that knock on the door. "Mr. Thompson, there's been an accident . . ."

One night Leo was at a friend's house for a sleepover and Sean was skating at Inner Space as word began trickling across cell phones and social media that they'd lost one of their own. At first, no one believed it, assuming it had to be some mean-spirited Internet rumor. Then came the confirmation: Michael was dead.

One of Sean and Leo's first Seattle skate pals, Michael

reminded me of my friend Don, transformed atop a skateboard into a different version of himself, a fearless and flowing dancer. He was an A student, a chubster amid the gang of spindly middle schoolers who'd come by our house after school to skate the backyard and alley. By high school he was smoking pot all the time, skating less, spraying graffiti, hanging with an older crowd. He dropped out and began experimenting with faddish drug cocktails, mixing prescription pills with the purple codeine-and-Promethazine syrup known among skaters and rappers as *drank* or *lean*—it makes you sway, slur, lean.

Michael's grandmother found him one morning in his bed, an open laptop by his side, with *Law & Order* queued up on Netflix. He was two weeks shy of sixteen.

Michael's overdose rattled the boys, and us, and echoed through the skate community. Mary and I worried Sean and Leo might use his death as an excuse to do something reckless, reactionary. Instead, the boys and their friends helped plan Michael's memorial service, a Spirit Keeper ceremony at a Native American cultural center beside a park called Discovery. Sean and Leo sat in the "inner circle" and toked on a peace pipe as a shaman smudged them all with sage smoke. The boys came home perfumed by sage and told us about the three-hour ceremony, how something spiritual happened to them all. They seemed so raw and vulnerable as they kept talking about their lost friend.

"He was such a pudgeball," Sean said.

"Yeah," Leo said. "But then he got so skinny, y'know? His whole face sunk in."

They both fell quiet, trying not to make each other cry. Then, as they had when Sean's classmate Joey died, and when their grandfather died, and during other times of sadness or strife, they went to meet up with friends at a skate park. I pictured them sitting at the rim of a ledge or bowl, skinny legs dangling against concrete, sharing more Michael stories and hiding their faces in their hands, and it just made me so sad and scared. He was only fifteen years old. Same as Sean.

Nate and others soon posted "RIP Michael" videos, compilations of Michael ripping tricks at Woodland and Inner Space, slo-mo shots of him laughing, high-fiving, flipping the bird. Then, in keeping with a skateboarding tradition I hadn't been exposed to, Sean and Leo etched "RIP MAC" onto their boards. Their friends all did the same. From that day onward, whenever my boys got a new deck, the first thing they'd do, almost ceremoniously, was scratch, carve, Sharpie, or graffiti *RIP MAC*.

We tacked Michael's obit and memorial card on the corkboard beside our fridge: "He was artistic and highly creative, loved the outdoors, music, jumping on his trampoline and skateboarding, a sport in which he excelled . . . Michael had friends from all walks of life and believed that we are all connected as people and one with the universe."

Seeing my boys and their friends once again mourn collectively, seeing them prop each other up during a painful time, affirmed my still-strong belief that their clutch of loyal (if sometimes troubled and troublemaking) friends were part of a community that embraced them and gave them an identity.

Or was I grasping for rationalization and hope, giving the skate life more credit than it deserved? On the surface: they were outdoors, exercising and practicing, not glued to a TV screen, living in a world that they'd created tucked inside one they didn't (or wouldn't) accept. One level deeper: they all coaxed each other to be more defiant, less compliant, to take more risks, to collectively step closer to the edge. They'd convinced each other that *that's where* they belonged—at the edge.

Michael's grandmother later told me that during his spiral downward into drugs, she felt he was "looking for something that just is not here."

It's not like we were pushovers. But after Michael's death, Mary and I began wondering: Were we doing enough?

Over the years, we'd tried every form of discipline. We grounded them. We banned TV and computer screens. We loaded them up with chores. We separated them from their friends. We confiscated their cell phones. We empowered teachers and counselors to keep them after school. And we frequently confiscated their boards.

We also talked to them (Mary), sometimes screamed at them (me), and they'd scream back (both). We encouraged, prodded, and just listened to them.

They didn't fear us. And I don't think we feared them,

though we did tire of the constant conflict. We wanted peace. We were running out of ammo.

At dinner, we'd be like two pairs of soldiers sharing a battlefield smoke during a holiday break in the action.

One thing we'd learned was that zero tolerance just didn't work in our family. The *no, no, no* stance usually backfired. Not only did it fail to achieve the desired results—they'd find pot if they wanted pot, for example, no matter the punishment—but it cleaved an unhealthy chasm between us and them. Not that we strived to be the kind of parents who were best friends with their kids. Mainly we just wanted to keep the lines of communication open.

So Mary and I developed a shifting, adaptive style of parenting and began experimenting with hands-off-the-wheel tolerance. We'd set boundaries, then back off and let them be free until they crossed the line, then we'd reset the boundaries, then retreat again.

That was more or less the tack we took on a spring break RV trip through Northern California and up the Oregon coast. When we dropped them at a skate park, or watched them walk into a forest of California redwoods, or onto sculpted Oregon dunes, we'd pretend we hadn't smelled that familiar scent coming from their backpacks, pretend we didn't know what they were up to. At a Mendocino campground I watched them climb high into a pine tree at sunset and thought, Well, why *wouldn't* they want to be a little buzzed? I still didn't understand their style of buzz, even as I exercised my own style, sipping bourbon and tending a campfire. But as long as it was just pot . . . maybe it was okay?

Mary had been reading a book I'd snagged from work, *Humboldt: Life on America's Marijuana Frontier*, thinking it might divulge some secrets of pot culture. As we drove through the infamous pot capital of Humboldt County itself, Mary kept reading passages aloud: "Pot farming was not only a way of life in the region, it was the foundation of the entire economy." During lunch at a steak house off Eureka's downtown square, two burly cowpokes walked in, all tawny skin, rough hands, ruddy cheeks. They passed our table on their way to the bar and left a pungent trail of dope in their wake. The four of us exchanged "did you smell that" looks, and laughed.

Driving toward home through Oregon, Sean got a call, and a job offer. We'd been encouraging the boys to find jobs, and Sean had applied for a position as a clerk at a local market. The manager wanted him to stop by the following week for an interview and to fill out some paperwork.

"Um, yeah, sure," Sean said. "That'd be fine."

Sean walked to the market after school, nailed the interview, and came home glowing and proud. But when the manager called the next day, she told Sean they'd decided to give the job to someone older, more experienced. They'd keep his name on file.

Weeks later, Sean called me at work. I was busy interviewing an author and couldn't pick up, so he kept calling, over and over. As usual, he didn't leave a message. The kid had an aversion to voice mail, ours and his, never leaving or listening to messages. I excused myself to call him back, worried that something was wrong.

"Dad?" he said. "I *got* it—I got the job!"

I had nudged Sean to go back and tell the store manager he was still interested, which he did, albeit reluctantly. The manager was impressed by his persistence and later told me: "That says a lot. Not many teenage kids would do that."

"Congrats, buddy," I told him. "I'm proud of you."

"I know, me, too. I'm psyched."

I returned to the author, who asked if everything was okay, and I was suddenly confessing parts of our story: the pot, the bad grades, the parental guilt, and now Sean's job, which was such a relief that I, as usual, could barely stop myself from tearing up. She was patient and generous. Most authors—like most skaters—knew something about failure and persistence. "Maybe it's best he got rejected," she said. "Things don't always work out the first time."

Helping Sean land a job—followed weeks later by Leo scoring a golf caddying gig—reminded me how vital work had been for me during high school. My parents always pushed Jeff and me to rake leaves, shovel snow, mow lawns, lifeguard, or babysit. I delivered newspapers at dawn at age twelve and one summer worked for an insurance agent at his home office, stuffing envelopes and licking stamps as the lonely old guy made me delicious toasted cheese sandwiches.

But the best jobs, maybe of my entire life, involved bricks and burgers.

Bricks: With my best friend (and skiing partner) Blaise, I lugged stacks of brick and block to the masons working for Blaise's dad. On weekends and during summers, high school through college, Blaise and I rose early, drank black coffee, two bony teens mixing batches of gray-sludge cement, pushing dozens of wheelbarrows of the stuff, getting sunburned and wiry-strong. We bummed cigarettes, learned to tell dirty jokes, took shit from foul-mouthed masons. We always had beer money.

Burgers: Shorter and kinder than Tony Soprano, my boss Vinnie ran his North Jersey greasy spoon, the Gibson Girl, the way Tony would later run his Bada Bing! strip club. Vinnie hired me as a dishwasher, then bumped me to prep cook, then to burger-flipping night cook, and finally took me under his wing to train me in the fast-paced art of slinging breakfast. Among the highest honors of my otherwise unimpressive high school years was getting tapped by Vinnie to sub for him on Sunday mornings.

In Jersey mobster parlance: I fuckin' loved that guy. Blaise's dad, too.

So when my own sons started earning their own cash, I finally felt that we and they were doing something right. I also hoped that some tough-love boss might knock some sense into them. Because, for the most part, they weren't responding to the proffered life lessons of teachers or parents.

An example of which: I'll spend the rest of my days flinching at phone calls arriving between 5:55 and 6:00 P.M. That's when we'd receive the near-daily automated calls from school. I'd see the number on caller ID and groan. When prompted, I'd reluctantly press "1" and listen to the recorded voice scolding me: "Your child [Sean or Leo] was marked [tardy or absent] from the following periods: [insert number(s)] . . . Please inform your child to get to class on time."

Most of these calls came at 5:57, and I'd bark "what!" and wait for the snippy, judgmental robot lady. I'd sigh with relief if it was just a tardy or two, but I'd growl at the words "marked absent," especially if that was followed (usually on sunny skate days) by "periods four, five, and six." That's when my shouting began, especially if it was both boys.

Remarkably, despite their spotty rates of appearance, many of my kids' teachers seemed to actually *like* them. Report card summaries read like "I hate to deliver bad news" equivocations—Sean was "a pleasure to have in class," but "frequently tardy"; Leo "shows creativity and originality," but "is missing a few assignments." Both boys would infrequently get the grades they (and we, and their teachers) knew they were capable of in class, then score in the upper tiers on state tests and proficiency exams. We had the same conversations so many times, to the point of parody: *your job is to go to class, get there on time, respect your teachers.*

The problem wasn't just the tardies, absences, and mediocre grades that littered their report cards like turds. It was the antiauthority attitude behind it all. Buried deep inside Sean's backpack—"a black hole," Mary called it—we'd find worksheets and essays that he'd completed but didn't feel compelled to turn in. Leo, if cornered after an egregious episode of absenteeism, would argue that people learned by doing things, not by listening to teachers read from textbooks or show movies.

"I'm not learning anything in that class anyway," he'd say.

"Well, no shit! You're never there!"

At their age, I can't say I loved high school, either. But I didn't *despise* the place, so I had no reference for my kids' avoidance and didn't entirely understand the depths of their disdain. Leo once texted me a complaint about a teacher with whom he'd developed a testy relationship: "I understand 'he's the teacher' 'he's in charge' 'blah blah blah' I understand all of that but you need to understand he has never once showed any respect to me. He's a bad person and an even worse teacher."

Mary and I would ask each other the same questions: Who's *fault* is this? Who should we be *mad* at? Our defiant kids? Their underfunded public school? *Ourselves?* Is it the pot smoking? Mary at one point started researching military schools and wilderness boot camps. "Why aren't you trying harder?" she'd angrily plead with her sons.

In weaker, boozier moments, I'd flog myself for not having the cash for private school or the guts for military school. One night after a shame-inducing robo-call, Mary and I went for a long walk and I told her I felt like a bad cowboy, the one who couldn't break his spirited horses, whose fences needed repair, the one the other cowboys snickered at.

As a former horseback rider, Mary tried to accept my cowboy analogy but refused to join in my misery. Sometimes she schooled me with her hopeful outlook, her resilience. As she often did anytime we paused on a run or a walk—or while brushing her teeth, or in line at the grocery store, or while cooking in the kitchen—my wife stretched and twisted and squatted, squeezing something productive from each in-between moment. "There's something in there, inside them," she said. "And we need to just wait for it to come out."

It'd take a few years for her to admit how worried she was at times, how she was not just waiting for her sons to blossom, but for her husband to stop acting so *mad*.

There were signs of her optimistic view right there in front of me. Sean's biology teacher once told me, with a hint of admiration, "Sean has his own interpretations of assignments. He negotiates. He reads what he wants to read, only pays attention to the things that interest him."

Just like the middle school vice principal who appreciated Sean's willingness to ask "why," the biology teacher found Sean's intractability both maddening and compelling. "He's a happy kid," another teacher said. "Very independent and bright. But he doesn't want to play the game. His attitude is: I know what I know, why do I have to prove it to you?"

It's not as if my boys weren't self-aware. In an essay on "values" (which he *did* turn in), Sean described the value that mattered most: *freedom*.

"Freedom is one thing I can't live without," wrote my son, who only wrote when he felt like writing. "It's one of the most important things in my life . . .

"At school, for me it is a constant fight for freedom. I'm always getting in trouble for pushing the limits of my freedom. Freedom is a value that can easily be taken away from you if you make the wrong decisions. Freedom is a great value but it has to be earned."

16

To cap off the school year, and celebrate the start of our fifth Seattle summer, Sean asked if he could host a backyard barbecue with friends. He wanted us to trust him. To treat him like a young man. No parents. And he wanted forty dollars for food.

Mary gave him twenty bucks and told him, "Don't burn the house down, Sean." Then we picked a happy hour spot close to home—close enough to hear the sirens.

When we got home, expecting a "Project X" house party, we found Sean and a dozen friends lounging out back, eating hot dogs and burgers that Sean was flipping on the grill. I knew a few of the kids and Sean introduced the others and I loved seeing my boy play host. He had things under control. No signs of weed or puke. I was so *relieved*. Sean had asked for our trust, we took a chance, he did what he said he'd do. He seemed proud, too.

And his friends? Even though I saw Max trying to hide a vodka bottle in a paper bag, they were nice kids, skater kids, high school kids, polite kids, just *kids*. Seeing them hanging out in my backyard, instead of as I imagined them—sucking on bongs, vomiting in the garden, fucking in the shower—demystified them. It made me feel like my boys were okay, we all were, a good family going through the typical ups/downs of high school.

Until I saw Leo.

Ashen faced. Swaying and slurry. More than just buzzed or baked, he looked awful. Totally zombified and on the verge of hurling.

"*Sean*—what's wrong with your brother?"

"Oh, um . . . I didn't want to tell you guys."

I tried not to freak, forced myself to take a breath and not break up the party.

Mary led Leo upstairs to the bathroom and I pulled Sean aside. Without needing to say it, Michael's death hung in the air between us.

Sean admitted that he'd been worried. He didn't know what Leo had ingested but suspected more than just smoke or drink. He'd been in a woozy, ghost-faced state all afternoon. Sean tried to help, making Leo drink water and eat yogurt and stay calm.

"Why didn't you just call us?" I asked, trying to keep my tone below a shriek.

"I thought I could handle it," he said. "I'm sorry."

Leo ended up hugging the toilet. He told us he'd eaten

a pot brownie on an empty stomach. Later, he backpedaled and said he just drank too much.

While Mary cleaned Leo up and put him to bed, one of Sean's friends grilled us each a burger while another volunteered to sit with Leo. Mary and I descended to the basement, drank red wine with our burgers, watched *Homeland*, and took turns checking on Leo. A typical American family.

Friday night, 1981: My mom picks up me and Dennis from a party. We're both drunk and high, not ready for the fun to end. Dennis is going to spend the night, but we decide to sneak out and head back to the party, which is miles away. From my attic bedroom we climb down from my balcony to Jeff's balcony one floor below, then drop onto the back porch. We plunge into the woods, hoping to find the trail that connects to a back road a mile away. We lose the trail and bushwhack the last stretch. We slip on a slope and tumble down and down until we reach the bottom and miraculously find pavement. We high-five each other, see headlights, stick out our muddy thumbs.

The car pulls over, but at the last second I realize it's a red Subaru wagon. *Shit.*

"Party's over, boys," my mom says through her rolled-down window—a line that enters the lore of my high school dumb-assery.

I'd think back on that night, and so many others like it—falling asleep in the bathroom after a Gibson Girl Christmas party; stealing Heinekens from the priests' kitchen at the rectory; driving drunk, stoned, and stupid—when my kids began pulling the same shit, ignoring curfews and our calls, sneaking out after we fell asleep, staying out until dawn.

Weeks after Sean's barbecue, we heard voices at 3:00 A.M. and found a party churning in the basement, starring my sons and six friends, two of them hurling. One of the girls had used a paintbrush to tattoo her feet and had left a trail of red footprints across the basement carpet. Another girl was slumped beside a bucket of nasty. Mary helped the two girls into her car and drove them home. As I cleaned up spilled beers and globs of vomit, Sean tripped over my bucket and sent puke-water flying. One of his friends, passed out on the couch, slept through my howls.

Another night, Mary and I were watching a movie when the boys came in and joined us, and the skunky weed-stank instantly filled the room.

"Are you *kidding* me?" I barked.

"Oh my god! Did you guys, like, roll around in pot?" Mary asked.

The boys stood there grinning, fiddling with their phones, and Mary continued: "Or . . . is one of you carrying a bag in your pocket because you don't know where to hide it?"

She meant to be sarcastic, but Sean looked up from his phone and replied: "Um . . . the second one?"

I tried to roll with it, to take deep breaths and not begrudge them for doing what teenagers did—what I had done. Still, that summer I started dreading weekends. Of all things!

Some mornings we'd hear the stories. About beach parties at Golden Gardens Park, keg parties at Carkeek Park or Discovery Park, or a "spodie," as my kids called their improv raves, in the woods behind Lower Woodland Skatepark. About cops showing up and the frantic escape with a keg—or at least an attempt to save the tap Max bought off eBay. About getting chased from strangers' homes when parents showed up and dialed 911. About missing the last bus of the night and walking home for miles. And those were just the stories they *told* us about.

For a while I used the "Find My iPhone" feature to track their locations—watching my sons as little blue dots moving from place to place on a digital map, usually someplace far from where they said they'd be—until they caught on and turned off the tracker.

Each night I'd lie there, wide awake—eleven, twelve, one—waiting and hoping for the creak of the back door hinge that was my signal to *breathe*. Instead, I pictured them huddled around a bonfire, passing around bottles, sharing joints and popping pills, maybe sipping cough syrup cocktails. Were they doing all the things I envisioned? Probably not, but it didn't help when they became entangled in their convoluted and far-fetched excuses.

"How'd you get home?" I asked when Leo scrabbled sloppily through the back door at 1:00 A.M.

"I, uh . . . walked."

"All the way from Carkeek?"

"A-*yup*."

The disconnect between our sleep-wake cycles created multiple time zones in our house. Sean would work an afternoon shift at the market, wait for Leo to get home from caddying, they'd play video games and make plans. Mary and I would be reading in bed and they'd come up to bestow good night hugs and kisses, then head out into the night.

"Just for an hour," they'd promise. "Back by midnight."

They'd get home at two and Mickey's guard-dog yaps would wake us. I felt like a sleep-deprived Bill Murray in *Lost in Translation* that summer. It'd take four Americanos to prime the morning pump. Groggy days would end with an *M* drink—Manhattan, martini, margarita—and at bedtime I'd sometimes summon "Mr. X," as Mary and I called our go-to sleep aid. We never abused Xanax. Just an occasional half tab, as in: "I needed a half last night." Far better than fog-brain Ambien. It calmed my thumping heart.

But how had summer become a season of dread? Did my parents fear summer nights as I now did? Far too often I felt tense and shitty, unstable and ashamed and afraid. I clutched at chest pains, jangly aches like a hooked fish beside my heart. I found it hard to breathe. Even during steamy hot nights I'd run around closing and locking windows while Mary slept peacefully, no visions of burglars or break-ins keeping her awake.

One night, with both boys out at parties, I lay awake thinking: I should be happy they've got so many friends. I should be trying to fool around with my wife. Instead, I imagined the boys spraying graffiti beside moving trains, jumping into a drunk kid's car. I sent a flurry of texts—"be safe!" "don't drink too much!" "don't get in a car!" Sean would always ignore these, and Leo would sometimes respond "you bet pops," but not tonight.

When I finally slipped into a fitful sleep, I had a dream: Sean was sitting on a wobbly plastic chair. He stood up, smashed the chair, picked up one of the legs, which turned into a fiery torch. He looked around him, then saw me watching. He smirked, slowly turned and plunged into a dark forest. His face emerged for a second and I yelled, "Sean! *Wait!*" He smiled again, his face illuminated by the torch, but turned back into the woods and disappeared. I yelled for him, but no sound came from my mouth.

Suddenly Mary was shaking me. I'd been shouting. I jerked awake, jumped out of bed, and ran down to check Sean's room.

Empty.

I spent the rest of the night texting him and waiting for a cop's knock on the door. By the time he showed up the next morning, full of apologies and excuses, my chest was banging so wildly I thought it was a heart attack. My breath was shallow and my heart juddered like a misfiring lawn mower. I kept checking my pulse. Finally, in a panic . . .

"Mary, something's not right."

I asked her to drive me to the hospital. It felt absurd. I was only forty-eight. I felt scared and erratic and so *tired*.

In the ER, after a few tests, all of them normal, I told the doctor about the boys and our puke-y summer and my fears for their safety. She nodded in sympathy. Or maybe pity. Her diagnosis: "chest congestion and atypical chest pain." And her discharge instructions made me feel so fucking *old*:

"You're to follow up with one of the cardiologists in the next 72 hours for a stress test."

On the drive home, we stopped by Sean's market to spy—it was becoming a habit. That morning he'd smelled like a barroom floor on a Sunday, and I felt bad for that day's shoppers. But I saw him now, smiling and chatting with customers. I looked back on my own version of sixteen, saw myself swaying at the Gibson Girl grill, nauseous and sweating out the previous night's beers, stepping out back to get sick behind the dumpster, then coming back to cook some nice family's postchurch omelets.

Sean finally saw me and forced a sheepish smile. I approached his checkout and pointed, asking with my eyes if I could get in his lane.

He shook his head, so I picked a different lane.

The next day was Father's Day. I was groggy and sad, rattled by the previous day's ER visit and hardly in a mood for the annual celebration of fatherhood. But Mary convinced me to get out of the house and come to yoga. We drove down the hill to squeeze our mats into a steamy, bamboo-floored room with other Sunday morning yogis.

I'd been doing yoga on and off for years, but Mary had lately become a devotee, and we'd both been trying to turn yoga into a soul-soothing habit.

I tried to focus on the instructor's advice about removing the bricks we carry, the things that prevent us from being who we want to be, who we're capable of being. In my case, the brick wall consisted of anger, anxiety, remorse, fear, shame, guilt . . . Lugging those bricks, the instructor said, only got in the way of our lightness, our happiness, our health. At the word *health*, Mary and I broke protocol and made eye contact, mid-asana, and shared a post-ER smirk.

"Want to make things harder?" the instructor continued. "Try holding your breath."

As I folded and twisted my body into triangles and right angles, downward dogs, warriors, and airplanes, I kept telling myself to *breathe*, dammit—you need to fucking breathe!

When it came to things I thought I could control—my career, my house, my marriage, my books, the stories I wrote—I was capable of optimism. Like most writers, I believed in what I was doing because I had to. But with my kids? It felt so out of my control. *They* felt out of control, and I had no control over *them*. Or . . . what if control wasn't the point? Maybe I needed to do the opposite, exert less control, simply think good thoughts, stay positive, remove the negativity from my life, just smash those bricks and breathe.

At times during my kids' embrace of the skate life, I'd try to reconnect with the carefree board rider I'd once been, the fearless kid whose mantra (sometimes too often) was "don't worry about it!" In recent years I had tried to get back into skiing, though I rarely managed more than a few days on the slopes each year. I'd tried a few times to learn to surf, though I came to prefer the safer stance atop a stand-up paddleboard. The cruelty of this particular Father's Day was realizing during the prone final minutes of class—in corpse pose—that my kids and their friends practiced that positive, brick-free, no-worries lifestyle every day.

Back home, despite the postyoga buzz, I wallowed in a Father's Day funk, even after Mary gave me a gift—a Hawaiian shirt for an upcoming family trip to the land of no worries. When the boys finally awoke, around two, they gave halfhearted apologies. Then they went skating. It wasn't until they came home to be fed that Mary reminded them what day it was. They felt bad. They hugged me. Mary told them about the ER visit, and they felt even worse.

I closed myself off in our bedroom and called my dad, wished him a woe-is-me Father's Day, then told him about what had been going on.

"Well," he finally said. "You do seem to give them a lot of freedom."

After I hung up, I sat thinking about that word. I thought . . . Isn't that what you and Pat gave us? Isn't freedom *good* for kids?

Thankfully, Mary rescued me from self-pity. The homemade card she gave me on that otherwise shitty day, a day after my ridiculous non–heart attack, would find its place among other letters and mementos in my lockbox, atop handwritten letters from Pat, Leo's baby teeth, tooth fairy letters, and the pins they'd removed from Sean's leg:

You are a fantastic father and a fantastic father can doubt himself during hard times. You are breaking these people into civilization, and they are not compliant people.

They are challenging, irresponsible, demanding, funny, careless, sweet, helpful, selfish, kind, obnoxious, emotional and sometimes really stupid. But mostly, they are loving—because you are loving. And right now they need their asses kicked by their loving parents.

Happy Father's Day. I love you.

A week after the Father's Day debacle, the annual Go Skate Day rolled around—a holiday they truly cared about.

This year, the boys and their friends planned to dedicate their day of skating to Michael, four months after his death.

School was already out, so they didn't need to skip this time. But there was one problem: Sean had to work an eight-hour shift.

I was at my office when Sean called—over and over until I had a moment to find a private spot and pick up. I walked to the hallway where I took personal calls, the same spot where Sean had told me about getting the job. Now he told me he wanted to call in sick.

"All my friends are going, Dad, I can't miss it," he said. "I need to be there—for *Michael!*"

I took a deep breath and told him that while I understood about Michael, the job was more important right now. It took ten minutes of negotiating, with more than one hang-up and call-back, until Sean reluctantly agreed to go to work.

On my way home, I stopped to spy on him again. As before, he was smiling and happily bagging groceries, chatting with customers and cashiers. I shopped until his shift ended, then spotted him in the parking lot collecting carts. He finally saw me and beamed, he puffed out his chest, showing off the name tag on his vegan-green work shirt, then hopped onto a cart and surfed it down the pavement . . . and it cracked me wide open. I started to choke, then weep, turning away and hoping he wouldn't see my stupid tears.

At home, Sean admitted that calling in sick had been a bad idea. He was invigorated and exhausted after his first-ever eight-hour shift. A little sad, too. About Michael. About missing Go Skate Day. About skating less and feeling his skills slipping away. "It's the only sport I love, and I'm losing my edge," he said. "It *sucks*."

I bit my tongue to prevent myself from offering the dumbest parent advice ever: *Welcome to the real world, kid.* But I did tell Sean that I knew what he was feeling. It had been two years since I'd started working at Amazon, and though I'd finished my fourth book—the Robert Ripley biography, which was published and nicely reviewed that summer, and even earned a cherished tweet from Leo: "whoever wants to see my pops on tv hes gonna be on the daily show tonight"—I missed my old life. I missed being at home with my boys, seeing them shamble home after school to make a mess of the kitchen. I missed being a stay-at-home dad, a writer dad, a skate dad . . .

I told Sean, "Skating will always be there for you, you're not losing your edge, you're doing the right thing." Advice as much for myself as for him.

PART 4
FLYING HIGH

got up to pee and looked out the bathroom window to see my heirs standing with their dog beneath the motion-detection light, talking and laughing—and smoking a bowl. It would've been cute if not for the drugs. I reached toward the window to bang, to bark out a "Knock it off!" But it was late, I was tired, and I didn't want another scuffle.

Back in bed I couldn't sleep, so I tiptoed down to the basement and found them sitting at Sean's desk, a huge bag of bud before them, refilling another bowl. When they saw me, their giggles stopped. I stood staring at them, hands and jaw clenched, unable to say a word. If I started to speak I knew I'd start screaming or throwing things or swinging.

So many times I'd walked away from my sons, pissed and ineffectual, hoping that my grim disappointment might have an impact, hoping they'd learn something from the hands-off freedom we gave them. But I'd built a head of steam, and felt fury and frustration shooting through my limbs. I took a step back and kicked at Sean's graffiti-covered bedroom door—harder than I meant to. My foot plunged through the cheap panel door and sent shards of graffiti'ed wood flying. I was stuck, hopping on one foot . . .

"What the hell are you two doing?!" I yelled like a nut. "It's a school night, you . . . you *stoners!*"

I wrenched my foot free, slammed the basement door, and let loose a straitjacket-worthy howl—"Fuuuuuuck!"—then popped half a Mr. X and slumped into a shitty sleep.

The next morning, I found a note Leo had slipped under our bedroom door, penned in red ink: "When a person does something wrong, pushing them away should not always be the solution . . . Resentment and getting angry will only turn our house into a stress-filled hell hole."

Downstairs on the kitchen table was a note from Sean, who said he needed to get his head together but was "someplace safe." I went to his room, but he was gone. I sat on his bed and read: "I love you so much, so, so, so MUCH! I've made my life way too difficult for myself and I'm not OK . . . I'm in pain in a lot of ways. I don't want you guys to hate me."

Anticipating the worst, I called in sick. Then I shakily texted and called Sean, texted and called his friends, as did Mary and Leo, but no one had seen him.

Finally, just before noon, Sean texted back. He'd slept in his car in a marina parking lot. He was safe. He was sorry.

I sat staring at my phone, trembly, relieved, sad. At that precise moment a calendar reminder popped onto the screen: "Maura B-day."

It was my sister's birthday. She would've been fifty-two. My anger melted away, but not my sorrow. I missed my sister. I missed my mother. And the distance between me and my brother and my father now felt every inch of the two thousand miles that divided us. Is that where my sons and I were headed, someday soon to be separated by the USA?

As we began muscling through another school year—Sean a junior, Leo a sophomore; ages sixteen and fifteen—I felt time accelerating. Sean had gotten his driver's license and Leo started driver's ed and I felt them both speeding toward a premature adulthood, hurtling away from me.

As a toddler, Leo had hated sleeping in his bed. He'd get up in the middle of the night and crawl onto the foot of our bed like a puppy. "I just want to be with Mommy and Daddy," he'd cry as we carried him back to his room. Being with Mommy and Daddy was no longer necessary. I'd get home from work and find him and/or Sean and some friends playing Xbox, sitting around someone's portable speaker listening to iPhone-propelled rap, munchies detritus everywhere, emptied chip bags, plates of panini crusts.

They'd see me and immediately grab their boards and flee. "Oh, hey, we were just heading out," they'd say, practically trailing cartoony curls of smoke, à la Pepé Le Pew.

In response to what seemed like an escalation in cannabis appreciation, I started stalking them online and one day found a music video on YouTube that Nate had made for a local rapper. I was impressed at what a great shooter/editor he'd become, graduating from his preteen skate videos to this professional-looking montage of a rapper and his posse, singing their praises to skating, bitches, ganja, and a Chevy El Camino.

> *All I ever wanted was shoes on the Chevy . . . skatin'*
> *through the 'hood*

Suddenly, Leo appeared on-screen, swimming inside a Seahawks sweatshirt, a slo-mo shot of him toking a blunt the size and color of a small dog turd, exhaling a gray plume. Later: Leo inside a skate shop, a small white kid swaying behind five older black kids rapping about life in the 'hood.

> *I grew up . . . right place wrong time*

I showed the video to Mary, who called Nate's mom to ask Nate to delete the Leo scenes. Leo was furious: "What's the big friggin' deal?"

Curious about what else Leo was up to on the Internet, I found his Twitter feed. This was before he and his friends migrated to Snapchat. On Twitter—a private account that I spied on with a stolen password, since he ignored my follow request—I discovered yet another version of my son.

- Excused maself from school today #fuckamonday
- The majority of my clothing smells like pot and cigs #grosss
- What would your family think if they saw your twitter lol

- Coolin it by myself, listening to the sounds in our world
- Idk what I would do without my brother

A writer friend (and former skater) once told me she viewed her own high school skating-and-smoking years as a "nihilistic exploration of my self annihilation."

Though Leo's tweets showed signs of nihilism—"I want to be out in the sun, so fuck your test mr smith"—I'd never considered street skating, cop conflicts, and a fondness for pot as flirtations with death. Risky, dangerous, self-destructive, and unproductive, for sure. But self-annihilation? Even after Michael's death, I just didn't see it.

Not until heroin became part of the equation.

Over the years I'd developed intermittent friendships with a few other skate dads. At holiday parties or an occasional happy hour or the rare school event, we'd share our latest stories, little Skate Dads Anonymous episodes of commiseration and confession. We were all frustrated by the constant smoking and drinking, each of us experimenting with different carrots and sticks, trying to find a balance between tolerance and obedience. But I don't think any of us imagined our boys would cross into opiate territory.

Then one of the dads, Robert, mentioned the house of another skater who had graduated from weed to cocaine to heroin. "That place is bad news," he told me, describing a scene of limited parental oversight and nightly parties. "You need to keep your boys away from there."

Months later I discovered why Robert had been so worried about that flop house: His son, Jack, had been hanging around there and one night was peer-pressured into putting a heroin-laced joint to his lips. A feeling he'd never known suddenly became the most important feeling of all.

Jack had been studious and athletic, a lanky-shy kid who played baseball and basketball, played drums in a band, got straight As. In high school he'd decided that none of that made sense, that he'd been faking it, playing someone else's games. When he discovered skating, he found his tribe, kids who spoke his language. Like my sons, Jack progressed through all the stages, from skate shoes to security guards to smoking. Then Jack delved one level deeper, and his parents were now frantically trying to pull him back.

They sent Jack to a wilderness rehab camp, but he escaped and hitchhiked back to Seattle, then moved out to live on a skate friend's couch. That night, Robert left us a message . . .

"Jack's really vulnerable right now," he said. "This could end badly."

Commiserating much later over burgers and beers, Robert recalled his terrors, using words that sounded familiar: "It was the most important job I'd ever had, and I was fucking it up." While he mostly flogged himself, he knew (as did I) that the disconnect between skate life and *life* life was to blame: "The real world isn't working for these boys."

Evidence of which stalked our family and now littered Leo's Twitter feed:

- Just bc I don't come to a class doesn't mean I'm dumb it means i'm smart enough to realize that what you teach me is irrelevant to my future
- Literally no one will EVER understand
- Wish I was a little kid again
- Can't wait to get out of high school and prove to my parents, teachers, and everyone else who doubts me that I can and will be successful
- Wtf am I doing wit my life

More than a handful of the boys' friends grappled with addiction, quitting high school, and WTF thoughts. I'd learn, in trickles of truth telling, that Michael hadn't been the only friend playing dangerously with Prozac, Ambien, Molly, and Xanax, which Leo later told me had become "the new heroin" among Seattle teens (prompting us to start hiding our "Mr. X"). "They already saw one friend die," Robert told me one night. "They think they're invincible."

The boys and their friends continued to think about, talk about, and remind one another about Michael. "RIP MAC"– decorated skateboards continued to tell a story of teen rebellion gone wrong, and my Internet stalking found a stream of fresh posts on Michael's Facebook page: "I love you, Michael," "I miss u so much," "I will always have a place in my heart for you." Nate's "RIP" video, dedicated to "a good friend and a talented skateboarder," kept racking up YouTube views, backed by Billy Joel's crooning.

*Slow down, you crazy child / You're so ambitious for
  a juvenile
But then if you're so smart / tell me why are you still
  so afraid*

On the anniversary of Michael's death, Leo tweeted: "I'll never forget when you taught me to kickflip homie. Cant believe its already been a year. Love you Michael. Rest easy."

With other friends teetering on the edge, with Robert's fears playing in my head, I started wondering if I'd recognize the danger signs, the subtle tilt when teen experimentation veered toward opiate-fueled doom. Was there a point when Michael could've been saved? If only someone had stepped in *right then and there?* How would I know if and when that moment arrived? Skating had been the thing that joined us as a family. Now it had introduced us to heroin, to rehab, to death. Skating contained the power to rip us to shreds.

Sean once told Mary: "I keep thinking the world is against me. But maybe it's me who's against the world." What saddened me was knowing that Mary and I represented the opposition, the other side. We were *the world*.

We'd never been big television watchers, although Mary had recently started binge-streaming *The Good Wife*, yelling at the screen like it was a football game: "Don't do it!" and "Yeah, baby, give it to him!" But lately we'd searched for a show that might provide some all-family entertainment, an effort to wrest the basement teen playhouse back to its intended purpose as *family* room. One night we all started watching *Game of Thrones*, but the boys eventually got bored and left, one and then the other.

My Spidey senses tingled, so I came upstairs and followed the spunk of weed wafting from our bathroom. I barged in as the boys tried to block me. "Wait! I'm taking a shower!" Sean yelled. Shoving my way inside, I found a bong-like contraption on the counter, a phallic fuck-you to our house rules and to our attempt at a family TV night.

In need of backup, I yelled to Mary, who came upstairs, furious at the intrusion to an otherwise mellow Sunday night.

"Right under our noses, *really?*" she yelled.

Leo launched into his now-familiar "what's the big deal" argument. Pot is legal in Washington. It's medicine.

"Not for you it's not," Mary countered.

Then Leo made the mistake of smirking. Mary wheeled on him, swatted him on top of the head—"Jesus, what's wrong with you?"—as Leo covered his head and yelled back, "What's wrong with me? Are you joking?" Mary charged and Leo curled into a ball. When Sean tried to intervene, Mary took a swing at him, too.

"Are you two crazy? What are you doing?" On the verge of losing her mind, she stomped off, back to the basement and the medieval TV lands of fire and ice.

I tried to calm things down, telling Leo that the correct response when you're busted smoking pot in your parents' bathroom is to apologize and beg forgiveness.

"Dad, I wasn't even *smoking*," he said.

I'd heard this inane argument before and would hear it in the months to come: "dabbing" involved the inhalation of heated-up hash oil vapors, so the boys felt justified in claiming they were *vaping* but not technically *smoking*.

Leo then dialed up some melodrama and woefully told me how he was stressed-out all the time, that his feet hurt, that he couldn't skate like he used to, that he was always being told what to do, at home and at school, that pot was the only thing that eased the stress.

While I wrestled with Leo's ridiculous rationalizations, Sean snagged the bong-like dabbing rig and fled.

For months Leo had been complaining about foot and ankle pain, which had been making it difficult to skate—something he'd been doing less, and feeling bad about it.

"You don't understand," he'd tell us. "It really *hurts*."

At one point we asked our family doctor to take a look, and at the same time to counsel Leo on the pot smoking. Our doctor, who had an admirable distaste for prescription drugs and an appreciation for patience and natural healing, gave Leo an exam, asked him what was happening in his life, and (at my sidebar request) talked to him about the pot.

He told Leo he had friends in their fifties who still smoked, some who grew and sold pot for a living and "make more than I do—so, you know, no judgment." But he'd also seen plenty of stoners who were sluggish and unmotivated, who didn't take care of their families. "They're unhappy, so they smoke more," he said.

Regarding Leo's feet, the doctor told us, "He's still grow-ing, so it could be growing pains. I think he'll be fine. He should stretch, maybe run or swim. We'll keep an eye on it."

Leo fidgeted but said all the right things, then on the drive home he grew agitated.

Among Mary's skills as a parent was getting the boys to talk by just being available. She knew face-to-face wasn't as effective as a slant approach, like a walk or a drive. On a re-cent drive, Leo had shared with her his thoughts on college, on studying graphic design, or maybe business or fashion, maybe designing skate shoes and clothes. But on my drive, instead of letting him open up at his own pace, I forced it, asking Leo about the doctor's pot discussion, which only ticked him off and shut him down.

"I know the repercussions, y'know. I've done the research and I'm aware of the consequences of my actions," he said. "I wouldn't do anything to my body that I hadn't fully re-searched."

He then went on about THC levels and parts per million and high-tech grow operations and rising standards, until I told him, "Okay, okay, I get it . . . No need to filibuster."

"That's not filibustering, Dad. Talking fast is a way to get my point across. I'm making a persuasive argument. It's a form of communication."

Finally, he calmed down and said he was more worried about his sore feet than about a doctor's advice on pot.

He did try stretching and running, but anytime he skated he'd come home in pain, his heels and ankles aching. He'd ice and soak them and even tried our doctor's home remedy:

a salve of mashed garlic and petroleum jelly, smeared on his feet and wrapped in plastic. But the pain continued, and Leo eventually stopped skating altogether.

On Twitter: "I'v lost so much touch with the skate community."

We finally took him to a podiatrist, whose X-rays showed early signs of a condition called "tarsal coalition," in which small foot bones begin fusing together. He suggested a specialist, whose CT scans confirmed what the first doctor suspected. The specialist walked into the exam room and his face said it all . . . "What's wrong?" Mary asked.

He explained the options, including a series of surgeries, two on each foot, to separate the fused bones and to repair Leo's flat feet, which had possibly been worsened by the bone fusions. As the doctor talked—and suggested starting with an orthopedic boot, immediately—Leo stared at the wall, lip shaking. On that drive home, Leo was crushed, scared, and *mad*. He faced spending all summer and half his junior year in and out of the hospital, in physical therapy, hobbling on crutches—and, unable to skate for as long as a year.

"Why?" he quietly asked from the backseat. "Why *me?*"

18

Weeks after his diagnosis, Leo turned sixteen. We threw a party with a few friends, gave him new skate shoes and a cake decorated with skateboarding action figures. That night, Leo celebrated Sweet Sixteen his way: a keg in the woods with a hundred of his closest friends.

We sensed he was up to something sneaky but wouldn't learn the details until the next morning, when I walked out the front door for the newspapers and saw the metallic glint of a spent keg shining beneath the rhododendron. Leo had slept at a friend's house, and when he came home later that morning, grinning like a goon, I asked how it went last night.

"How'd it go?" he said, pulling a roll of cash from his jeans, unfolding it and waving it in my face. "That's how it went, Pops. That's stripper money right there."

Proud of his successful bash, he couldn't keep it to himself. He told me about scouting a wooded location behind

Lower Woodland Skatepark, announcing the party to friends via Twitter ("8:00 KEG @ WOODLAND"), charging $3 per cup—apparently a cut-rate price for a keg party—which helped lure a throng of teens to his birthday bash. I later sneaked a peek at his Instagram pics and it was indeed an admirably rowdy mob.

Refolding his bills, Leo told me: "The thing about a keg, Dad? It's an *investment*."

It was a testament to the weirdness of being a skate dad that, at such times, I'd claw once more for signs of hope. My son's an entrepreneur, an entertainer, a salesman. Or, as Mary helpfully put it, "Didn't Tom Cruise get into Princeton at the end of *Risky Business*?"

The next day Leo asked for a ride to Carkeek Park, where he was going to meet up with friends at an abandoned concrete slab they called Helipad.

I let him drive, and he parked at the trailhead at the southern edge of the park, the secret back entrance at the north end of Mary Street.

I didn't want to let him go just yet, so I locked the car and started walking down the trail with him, watching him step gingerly over rocks and roots. Along the way, we talked about how he knew every corner of that park, spodie spots like Helipad, "Big Tree," the railroad tracks, and the beach. Incapable of employing Mary's method—walk, wait, listen—I launched into my standard "don't smoke/be careful" speech and was about to add a "don't drink too much" nudge, but caught myself. I knew I'd become a nag. And though I never aspired to be the "cool" dad, I never wanted to be a noodge, either. So I shut my mouth and kept walking. Even when I heard the clink of bottles in his backpack.

Leo finally stopped—"Okay, Dad. That's far enough."

We hugged, swapped I-love-yous—or, as Leo put it, "I McLove you, Pops"—and I watched my backpacked boy wind his way down the slope. He knew I was watching and tossed one last thumb-and-pinky overhead shaka wave without looking back, then rounded a corner and disappeared into the trees.

For a moment, I thought of myself at that age, roving and exploring; always on the move, always with friends; scheming and crossing lines, getting into trouble and pulling back; but always with a destination, a plan, a pack of pals—and, if lucky, a six-pack.

On a beautiful sunny evening, my kid was walking on sore feet to see friends, to catch a buzz and watch the sun go down across Puget Sound. How could I reject that?

As I trudged back to the car, I realized how much of my stress and anxiety was lashed to moments like this—to my fear of letting my boy walk down a path alone.

Despite my complicated feelings about returning to office life—to quote Leo: #fuckamonday—one of many perks at Amazon was access to lots of books. Boxes and padded envelopes arrived daily, attempts by publishers and authors to get my and my colleagues' attention, to score a review or get selected as a Best Book of the Month pick.

A surprising number of these books were about parenting, adolescence, fatherhood, and raising boys. I'd quietly slip those titles into my backpack, and they began piling up bedside and filling bookshelves: *The Secrets of Happy Families*, *The Smartest Kids in the World*, *All Joy and No Fun*, *Masterminds and Wingmen*, and, my least favorite title, *Do Fathers Matter?* I even bought a few classics of the canon: *The Wonder of Boys*, *Raising Cain*, *The War Against Boys*, and *Parenting Teens with Love and Logic*.

Sample guilt-inducing snippet, from *Battle Hymn of the Tiger Mom*: "schoolwork always comes first . . . an A-minus is a bad grade." Yellowed by my highlighter in *The Teenage Brain*: "best tool as they enter and move through adolescence is to be good role models. If there's anything I've learned with my boys . . . they were watching me."

My boys were indeed watching. One day Leo saw me reading on the couch, highlighter in hand, sipping whiskey. (*Role model?*) He picked up a book from the coffee table, read the title—*How to Raise Drug-Free Kids*—then dropped it like it was poison. He started to walk away, but devoted Instagrammer that he'd become, turned back, whipped out his phone, and took a picture, then typed some snarky caption (which I found years later: "my parents have had a little trouble adjusting to my 'adolescence'").

If Leo's reaction to such books was often bemusement,

Sean's was disgust. He once left a note inside *How to Raise Drug-Free Kids*, scrawled in Sharpie: "SERIOUSLY?!"

The book that most rankled Sean was *Surviving Your Child's Adolescence*, filled with my highlights and underlines in sections on "lazy teenagers" and "the age of thankless parenting." As with other such books, I was searching for secrets but mainly feeling scolded. Sean once hid that book in my closet, and I found it months later with a rant of a note describing how much it pissed him off, "mostly because I don't think you're gonna get any help from a book on how to raise a child you've already had for 16 years."

My son had a point. Was I really learning anything from books by strangers? Or was it parental masochism? I never actually got too far into any of these, often bailing after fifty pages, sufficiently chastised and chastened. The author of *Surviving Your Child's Adolescence* blamed "indulgent parents" for allowing their kids to believe that "self, fun, and now are all that matter in life." (No?) Such books seemed to be written for other parents, *tiger* parents, those able to micromanage or crack a whip.

By now Mary and I had at least learned the limits of zero-tolerance threats and punishments, schedules and limits, and advice containing the word *don't*. We'd made thousands of attempts at structure and obedience, usually leading to confrontations that left us all emotionally spent. Such efforts rarely seemed to make a dent. They'd apologize for their transgressions, stoically submit to their punishments, then do it again, and again . . . As *All Joy and No Fun* put it, teens tormenting their parents ranked among the oldest of human stories—"wronging the ancientry," per Shakespeare, was practically a teenager's *job*. Said the Bard: "I would there were no age between sixteen and three-and-twenty."

Sean stayed out until 4:00 A.M. and came home with a girl. They rattled around the kitchen, making ramen noodles, banging pots and giggling until Mary went downstairs and cornered him. "I want to just punch you in the face right now, Sean." I once scolded Sean for stealing one of my beers, and he apologized—for not recycling. Then there was the night Sean and friends drank more than half of the most expensive bottle of bourbon I'd ever owned, and probably ever would—George T. Stagg, a gift from a writer friend.

It sometimes felt like a war without end, our own Middle East–style standoff. Them: *We want to have fun!* Us: *Just play the game!* Us (via text): *Be home by 1!* Them: *(. . .)*

They'd become so instinctively opposed to rules, restrictions, and expectations that we realized we could spend years in turmoil and look back on only shouting, anger, and sadness. So Mary and I continued to experiment with our UN peacekeeper approach, grudgingly tolerating their defiance and fuckups, their messy slog toward self-rule, even as we worried constantly that every inch of freedom we gave them might carry them an inch closer to their annihilation.

"What if they veer too far outside the mainstream?" Mary once wondered aloud. "What if they don't find their way back?"

We didn't easily adopt our free-range approach. Some days

it was hands off the wheel, other days hands in the air, or hands around their throats, or heads in our hands . . . It veered wildly, depending on the situation and our mood. Like a relief pitcher, we kept changing our delivery. The author of *Drug-Free Kids* scolded: "The key to Parent Power is being engaged in your children's lives." But . . . we *had* been engaged, we were *still* engaged. Yet we had limited Parent Power, and our kids were hardly drug-free.

To paraphrase Sean: our methods seemed flawed. After getting reprimanded for some pot-related infraction, he left a note on the kitchen table, addressed to *weirdos*:

"STOP READING BOOKS ON HOW TO RAISE ME."

When they were younger, being their dad felt so much easier, so lacking in consequence—I wasn't trying to get it right, I was just having fun. They wanted to hang with me, and I usually knew what they wanted: playgrounds, skate parks, movies, skate shoes, lunch, a new skate deck, a skate-themed T-shirt. But what was my role now? What, as they said at my day job, was my *value prop*? I wasn't really the enforcer anymore, or the boss. Nor was I entertainer, driver, motivator, or confessor. What could I really *do* for them now? What could I say that wouldn't totally piss them off?

Skating had brought us close, kept us together, and now it'd been replaced by smoking, and we no longer had solid common ground. It made me feel so separate from them, so much *older*. When I was in San Francisco for work, I'd be drawn to Dogpatch, the neighborhood near that Third and Army skate spot. In Los Angeles, I'd find myself jogging toward the Venice Beach Skatepark. Sometimes I'd realize how much I'd let their skating define me, how I'd co-opted their obsession and made it my own.

One night I watched Sean playing Grand Theft Auto in the basement, stalking Venice Beach. "Go to the skate park," I told him, remembering that day we lost him during our road trip. In a rare moment of compliance, Sean guided his on-screen thug to the skate park, then heeded my suggestion to pummel a surfer in a wet suit, and we both cracked up.

Drinking a Manhattan and catching up on the *New York Times* one Friday night after work, I came across a story about how the trendy Paleo lifestyle applied to parenting: "Instead of cello lessons, let the kids run wild in the woods." I called out to Mary, who was chop-prepping dinner stuff in the kitchen . . .

"Hey, guess what? We're *Paleo* parents!"

That article would join others in a folder labeled sk8 clips, which had grown fat with stories about three topics: skateboarding, parenting, and pot.

A sampling of headlines captured the confusing state of modern fatherhood:

The Case for Delayed Adulthood
Pot Use on Rise in High Schools

Parental Involvement Is Overrated
Skateboarders Defy Court Order to Race Down Broadway
Troubled Teens Make More Successful Entrepreneurs
New Pot Laws Have Parents Worried about Effect on Kids
Excessive Arguing with Family May Lead to Early Death
The Case for Free-Range Parenting

I would read Mary a few lines about the benefits of maturing slowly, the confidence-inducing power of letting kids make their own decisions, and how "prolonged adolescence is actually a good thing." Per the *New York Times*, delayed adulthood fostered "novelty-seeking and the acquisition of new skills."

One article cited a UCLA study that found American kids spent 90 percent of their leisure time at home, and I realized . . . Not ours. Not even *close*.

Another op-ed writer opined that a parent's job was fairly simple: "They should set the stage and then leave it." Mary and I would high-five each other and toast the *New York Times* for endorsing our parenting style—"Maybe we don't suck after all!"

Then again, it was around this time that Sean got assaulted by a mob of drunk thugs at a beach party, pummeled in the head with his own skateboard.

My little boy's face had a purple knot above his eye, a deep gash across his forehead. His nose was mashed and swollen, his lip split in two places. An angry red lump grew behind his ear. Dried blood flaked from his hair and ears, peeling off like old paint. His white T-shirt was splotched rusty brown.

We were in the kitchen. I was about to leave for work when Sean limped up from his basement bedroom to show me his injuries.

"What the *fuck?*" I barked, dropping my backpack and reaching out to touch him, but he pulled back and winced.

"Careful," he said, then showed me the rest: bloody gouges on his arms, a shredded shoulder, a crooked finger, a cut and swollen ankle.

He looked like he got run over by a truck—worse than when he *did* get hit by a car.

"Jesus *Christ*, what the . . . why didn't you *call* me?"

"Wrong place, wrong time," he said, trying to sound hard but his voice cracking a little.

Driving to the ER, he told me he'd been at a Golden Gardens beach spodie when a group of "gangbangers" showed up looking for trouble and started a fight. One of them mistook Sean for another kid and jumped him. Sean curled into a ball and tried to protect his face as six guys took turns kicking and punching him. Someone snatched Sean's skateboard and slammed him in the head. Then did it again. One of the gangbangers finally intervened, screaming that they were assaulting the wrong kid. And they all fled.

We spent three hours at the ER—the same room Mary and I visited last summer, the day before Father's Day, with me clutching my throbbing chest. God, I hated hospitals. I thought I'd already paid my dues over the years: my brother, my sister, my mother, my sons, myself. And now I was worried about the possibility of Leo's foot surgeries, imagining Mary and me in waiting rooms, retrieving our cut-up, drugged-out little boy. But here I was, back beneath those too-bright lights, waiting for some doctor to take charge.

After X-rays, MRIs, and other tests, a cheerful young ER doc gave his reassuring verdict: Sean was fine. Maybe a mild concussion, but no internal bleeding, no broken bones, just battered and bruised, lumpy, gashed, and embarrassed. Then a social worker came in and asked me to step outside, so she could talk to Sean . . . "Alone, if that's okay." It took me a second, but then I got it—"Young man, did your father hurt you?"—and it shamed me, even though I had nothing to be ashamed of. Or did I?

Back home, as if releasing a pressure valve, Sean told me about other incidents. About the night a gun fell from some punk's pants. About the night he and his friends left Golden Gardens and heard gunfire, then sirens, and learned the next day that a woman had been shot.

"I dunno, I think maybe I'm a little too comfortable being close to danger," Sean said, though I wondered if it was true or something he wanted to believe.

"I don't always make the best choices," he added, then qualified it with a line that unnerved me. "But it's not like I'm susceptible to peer pressure. I'm susceptible to *curiosity*."

Sean napped that afternoon, then we made dinner and

watched a movie. Leo was at a friend's house that weekend (it was spring break), and Mary was traveling in China for business and was spared all of this. I was reluctant to call her, to describe once again how one of our kids had put themselves in harm's way.

When Sean came to my room to say good night, he told me, "I think the worst part of it all is . . . I lost my skateboard."

It was a short cruiser board with fat wheels that Mary had bought him. Like all of his boards, it had "R.I.P. MAC" etched into the grip tape. One of his attackers had tossed it onto the bonfire.

"I loved that little board," he said, and that's when he broke down and cried.

A week later, Mary was still in China, so the boys and I packed the boards and took a road trip north to Whidbey Island.

Sean's wounds had healed into bruise-hued rainbows of purple and yellow. I let him drive the first half, then let Leo test out his driver's permit from the ferry terminal to our rental. After we checked in I let the boys take the van to a nearby skate park and I sat talking with the owner of our cottage, an energetic woman named Joy who had just lost her dog to cancer and seemed happy to have a stranger to chat with.

Joy was impressed that I'd convinced my teen sons to come away for a weekend. I told her they'd always been good road trippers and described a few of our adventures: Hawaii, Costa Rica, Puerto Rico, Mexico, ski trips, skate trips, and that cross-country adventure.

"That's nice," she said. "I wish I'd done more of that."

After a few quiet moments looking out onto Useless Bay, she turned to me and got serious.

"They're not ours, you know. You have to let them go."

Both of Joy's kids were in their late twenties and had moved away. She said their teen years had been the worst. She was *so* glad they were behind her.

"Sorry," she added, realizing I was in the midst of those years.

I told her one of my nagging worries was that we had let them go too soon, that we'd let them be *too* free.

"Well . . . Better to give them freedom now than have them try to learn it in their twenties," she said. "No matter what, they come back to you . . . eventually."

Prying deeper into my head, she continued, "But they don't really need us, you know? They need to learn on their own. All you can really do is love them."

I nodded, sipped my beer. She sensed what I was thinking . . .

"And you can't be so hard on yourself!"

19

Mary and I unrolled our yoga mats, side by side, surrounded by Lycra'd strangers, all of us hoping to stretch and perspire away our worries. We were relieved to see our favorite instructor take charge, a New Yorker named Rob who played surprisingly yoga-friendly music: the Cure, Miles Davis, the Police, and Mary's favorite, Led Zeppelin.

Rob's classes often felt tailored for parents of skater teens, full of advice about patience, tolerance, and self-forgiveness. "Judge not," he'd tell us. He'd quote Jefferson: "The boisterous sea of liberty is never without a wave." I'd look over at Mary, who'd roll her eyes, meaning, *No shit*. It came as no surprise to learn that Rob had been a skater. He often seemed to have just the right message or song for our anxiety du jour. Some tunes seemed like inside jokes for skate parents: "Riders on the Storm"; Beastie Boys; Bob Marley.

Toward the end of one class he read a passage about our spiritual journeys being so full of "twists, turns, surprises and upsets, much confusion and stumbling until we reach a moment of clarity . . . but we usually learn best when we're a bit vulnerable."

At the word *vulnerable* I turned to see Mary looking my way. *No shit.* Rob kept reading as Mary and I held eyes: "Trust that the lesson will reveal itself to you when it's time."

As we sometimes did during class, Mary and I reached across and briefly touched hands.

"Other people may be there to help us, teach us, guide us along our path," Rob said, closing his book. "But the lesson to be learned is always *ours* . . .

"Stay present for this one perfect moment. Be. Here. Now. And *breathe*. It's amazing what can happen when you just let go and trust that the universe will catch you."

I looked up at the sun peeking through the skylight, closed my eyes, and breathed.

With the end of the school year crashing down on us, Mary and I found ourselves increasingly drawn to bamboo-floored yoga studios—our version of the skate park, atop mats instead of boards. And it came as a relief, nearing fifty, to find yoga teachers as ideal mentors, after so many years of resisting or defying mentorship. And for good reason.

I was once an altar boy. After a field trip to the Jersey Shore I was waiting for my mom to pick me up when the tubby young priest who'd trained us altar boys guided me behind the bus, gave me a hug and a sneaky little kiss on the lips. He was later accused of molesting two of my classmates and got shipped off to Arizona.

I once had a football coach. A buzz-cut ex-marine with whiskey breath who chain-smoked Marlboro Reds, who shoved and tripped us, called us pussies and candy-ass cunts.

I once had a high school teacher. He lived for a spell in the coaches' locker room, where he impregnated a classmate and later posted anti-abortion leaflets on our lockers.

So. With a cur-mouthed coach and two rapists as early mentors, I'd developed a tainted view of authority from a young age. I knew it, too. I sometimes oozed a subtle disdain for leadership and wasn't always a compliant subordinate, which editors from my early newspaper days could verify.

But I'd had plenty of positive role models, too. My friend Blaise's dad, the hardworking German mason, taught me to rise early and work hard, and Vinnie, my Italian mentor at the Gibson Girl, taught me to cook for customers as if they were family. A high school English teacher once told me, "You're a good writer," and in college my Irish lit professor, a boozy Jesuit priest named Quinn—who on day one asked us, "Are you lovers or are you *fuckers?*"—reinforced the simmering conceit that the writer's life was for me.

And my parents? They'd coaxed me into finding jobs from an early age, encouraged my interest in music and reading and writing. But as hands-on coaches? They mainly expected me to figure out my own shit. As my mom always said: "It's your life, NT."

Maybe it was a New Jersey thing, or a stubborn Irish

thing, but I simply learned to do life my own way, from paying most of my college tuition to living in five different cities across my first five postcollegiate years, to choosing a partner as stubbornly self-reliant as me.

But now, with boys of my own, it troubled me to realize that by not learning to be coached, I hadn't learned to *be* a coach. I rarely felt capable of inspiring or enlightening my kids, so I brought home books, hoping that some fantastical story would have an impact, that J. K. Rowling, Suzanne Collins, George R. R. Martin, or Stephen King would slice into their souls the way Vonnegut, Tolkien, Hemingway, John Irving, Flannery O'Connor, Joyce Carol Oates, Haruki Murakami, and Stephen King did mine.

In my journal one night I wrote: "It seems all I do is punish or talk or yell. How the hell do I inspire, motivate, teach, help? I'm always trying to change their lives. Do they need changing? Or does it make them feel bad that I think it does? Am I a bad coach? Or are they uncoachable?"

This inner/penned dialogue went on for quite a few pages in my chicken scratch . . . "What makes a good dad good, and a bad dad bad? Are they insufficient young men (at least so far), and does that make me an insufficient mentor? Or are they beautiful, vital young men, finding their way, and I'm just a dick for not admiring them as they are?"

Breathe.

Mary wasn't someone who'd been easily coached, either. The youngest of five, she preferred riding horses, often alone, to the more typical team sports. Like me, like her sons, she usually (and still) followed her own rules. (*Mary, Mary, quite contrary . . .*) We'd clearly passed our don't-tell-me-what-to-do sensibilities on to our kids. We knew this much.

Then again, Mary seemed to sense, better than I, when the boys needed some nonjudgmental parental support, or simply a no-expectations walk or drive. Mary's version of hands off was truly hands off, while mine was like a badly wired lamp, on and off, on and off. Mary knew how to be there when her sons needed to talk. Not to lecture or nag, but just be present and patient. She also provided an optimistic counterweight to my everything's-fucked attitude.

My spouse never envisioned the awful things I did. She didn't check the boys' bedrooms when she got home from work, bracing for disaster, terrified of finding them on the floor, slumped on their bed, drowned in puke. I hated that my mind was even capable of such dark imaginings, that I tormented myself with the terrible what-ifs.

But Mary? She believed in her sons. Though she sometimes wondered if all the skating had been a mistake, and whether we might have done things differently—moved around less, sent them to private school, penned them in a little *tighter*—she knew our kids were good people, just as she knew they were capable of good things. Eventually.

"We just need to be patient," she'd say, sounding like our yoga instructor. "We just need to create the right environment and hope for the best."

Or: "They don't really want to be part of 'the thing.' It's a mellow rebellion in some ways."

Or: "I'm feeling more confident. I don't think they're going to be homeless or anything. It's just going to be slow."

Yet, when a writer friend asked Mary if she wished things had gone down differently, she snapped, "No! I wouldn't want them to be anyone else."

Raising two boundary-pushing boys required teamwork. And by now we'd become a better team—more in sync, more stable, more resilient.

It fascinated me that our marriage hit a groove at the two-decade mark, coinciding with the slow emergence from the teen-raising high school years. A steady dual income and a nice house sure helped. But so did our day-after-day marital routines, which kept us grounded and close, strengthened our half of the two-on-two household dynamic.

Sunday morning yoga became one such sacred rite, preceded and/or followed by an ink-fingered session with the *New York Times*, sipping our pot of half-caf, reading obits and op-eds to each other. (Mary's faves: Vows and Corner Office; mine: the Book Review.) Another rite: on Friday nights, we'd get home from work and dive into our own two-person happy hour, mixing cocktails and grilling dinner while listening to the rockabilly show on KEXP, followed by a dog walk and a TV show binge session. And . . . with any luck, we'd slip upstairs . . .

We spent time with friends, of course—and with our boys, when they let us—but we had no problem hunkering down. It felt good to be at home, anchored and available if someone needed us (which they often did). Our rituals came to matter in ways that surprised me. They became part of a continuum of our marriage, our family, our life.

Other routines: a three-mile loop run, down to the waterfront and up the steep steps; long walks with Mickey, during which Mary would smell all the roses, pluck her stalks of rosemary, and scold me for hating nature; strolls through the Sunday farmers' market, people-watching amid our increasingly hipper-younger Seattle neighbors. Though we infrequently ventured into the mountains, our urban hikes could last hours. We'd explore the same city parks the boys used as party spots, walking railroad tracks and industrial ghost blocks much like they had, but in our own weird way. We'd take a one-way, miles-long hike into some 'hood, then call the boys for a ride home, or take Uber or Car2Go.

We usually promised each other not to talk about the kids but rarely succeeded. Still, life was strangely, slowly becoming less about them, more about us. A visiting brother-in-law once teased, "Do you hold hands when you run?" We did not, and we weren't a lovey-touchy couple. I'd refer to her as my "first wife"—a term I once used on a birthday cake—and I was her "current husband." If I told her I loved her, she'd sarcastically offer, "*thanks*"—or just "ditto."

One Friday after work we sipped our end-of-week drinks, listened to the radio, made dinner, then walked the dog to our neighborhood's downtown strip.

"Did I get fat?" asked my wife, who at fifty was probably slimmer than when we'd met.

"Yes, a little," I told her.

Mary found a lavender bush, snapped off a bud, rubbed it into her palms, threw the dregs at me, put her palms to her face, inhaled, and said, "I *hated* high school."

"Really?" I asked, then tried her lavender routine, sniffed at my sweet-smelling hands . . . "I thought you had fun in high school?"

"Not mine. *Theirs.*"

We stopped at the movie theater where Leo had recently gotten a job. Seeing him at the popcorn machine, so cute in his name-tagged uniform, I was tempted to take a photo— Leo had turned me onto Instagram. But Mary saw me reaching for the phone, read my mind, shook her head. She knew Leo would be embarrassed or pissed.

Back home, after a few binged episodes of *Orphan Black*, Mary said: "Life would suck without you."

"Thanks," I said.

I waited a minute, then told her, "All I need is you, y'know."

"Me, too."

The two of us deeply asleep as the phone trills at 2:00 A.M. Few sounds are as shrill and awful as a ringing phone after midnight.

Tonight, it was the call I'd feared for years.

"Is this Mr. Thompson?"

"Who is this? What's *wrong?!*"

"Officer Elias. Seattle Police Department. Are you the father of Leo Thompson?"

Fuck. In a quavering voice, I croaked the terrible question: "What . . . is he . . . is Leo okay?"

The officer assured me that Leo was, in fact, alive. But he was drunk and mouthy and in trouble. My son had been busted at a party in an abandoned school and was being detained– the only one among thirty-plus kids they didn't release—due to alcohol on his breath, paint-splattered hands, and "frankly, because of his disrespectful attitude."

I drove to the address Officer Elias gave me and found my five-foot son standing on a corner encircled by *eight* cops. When Leo saw my car he shot both hands into the air, holding up his number one fingers, like John Cusack in *Say Anything* but without the boom box. Officer Elias reached out to shake my hand, and I took it, then felt guilty. The beefy cop explained that a gang of kids had been inside the school, spraying graffiti and drinking, that they'd found paint on Leo's hands. Instead of apologizing, Leo had argued, and Elias said he had no choice but to hold him. "If I let him go? And he got killed? That'd be on me," he said.

On the way home, Leo launched into his indignant, lawyerly filibuster mode, bitching about how the cops were all wrong, that he wasn't spraying graffiti, that they'd harassed him because he'd dared to speak up and defend himself. This all occurred not long after Michael Brown had been shot and killed in Ferguson, Missouri, and I told Leo about trigger-happy cops and innocent people getting shot all the time. (Sadly more so in the years to come.)

At home, still jacked up from the night's excitement, Leo

begged to go back out with his friends. We refused, but after we fell asleep he snuck out anyway.

Next morning at yoga, the instructor led us into twisted triangle and joked, "This will help rinse out last night's bourbon and bad decisions."

Breathe, Neal, breathe . . .

In the fall of 2014—Leo's junior year, Sean's senior—both boys began taking community college classes, even as Leo insisted he'd be successful with or without college.

A program called Running Start allowed our kids to earn credits that applied toward high school and college. Sean passed the entrance test with a 91 percent and Leo soon after got an identical score. Ours weren't the only boys in our circle empowered by DIY schooling options. Many of their friends replaced high school with Running Start, cobbling together a mix of high school and college classes—school on their terms. By the spring of 2015, Sean would be done with high school entirely, opting for a mash-up of Running Start classes, a one-on-one math tutor, and online college courses. Proud of his unique educational path, he scribbled on one of his *three* report cards: "I are smart."

One night Mary and I were cooking fish when Sean asked for help with an essay he was writing for his English 101 college class. The topic: his relationship with literature.

"I think I'm going to write about how you being an author has influenced me—as a writer and a reader," he said.

I had to walk outside so he wouldn't see me cry. We had

so rarely discussed my writing, and I was pretty sure he and Leo hadn't read any of my books. So I felt like an asshole, *again*, for underestimating him/them. I later found Sean's three-page essay, which humbled me with its analysis of my writing career and his budding interest in storytelling.

"Being the son of an author, I was always taught proper grammar and received a lot of help with my writing," he wrote. "So I guess I was dealt a good hand when it comes to learning how to write, but also learning how to articulate and be clear with what I had to say, whether it be text or speech."

As we neared the tail end of high school, both boys managed to work their free-will expressions—on skateboarding, freedom, justice—into their writing assignments.

Leo, in an essay on *The Little Prince*: "Narrow-mindedness gets you nowhere in life. All great minds have one key advantage: they think outside the box, they push the limits of what can be done. That is what makes them so great. *The Little Prince* represents the open-mindedness of people and the desire to explore and discover . . . it shows the importance of exploration."

Some days I wondered whether I was teaching them anything, or if they were teaching me.

At times I started entertaining the idea that the boys were settling down and growing up—that, as a family, we all were.

There were signs. Like Leo's handwritten "Life Priorities" list, which I found while snooping in his room for drugs:

- Get into college
- Stay happy
- Find out what I want to do in life
- Start earning my own money
- Continue skateboarding

I wanted to pencil in one more: *Stop smoking pot!* But we had some work to do on that front.

Thankfully, our family doctor weighed in—again, at my request—forcing Leo to discuss his pot smoking during a checkup. He told Leo that as a teenager his brain was soaking up the world, taking it all in, learning and experiencing.

"If you smoke, you shut out the world," he said. "You deny yourself the opportunity to appreciate and swallow up all the world has to offer. There's a haze between you and the light."

That night Leo came to our room and sat on the bed, and I felt myself reaching for the same nagging questions about school, homework, grades, friends, and jobs, ready to offer advice, wisdom, or warning. Instead, I kept my mouth shut. And that's when he opened up. He'd been thinking about what the doctor had said but disagreed that he was closed off to the world. He considered himself more open-minded than many of his peers. He felt mature. He had plans.

"It doesn't matter what my grades are right now," he insisted. "I have a drive inside me. I want to succeed. No matter what, I *will* be a success."

Still . . . he was thinking about smoking less, and exercising more. He'd been taking three-mile walks with Mickey, and stretching his aching feet. He'd started lifting weights, doing pull-ups and push-ups in the basement, asking us about nutrition and eating better. He'd even started running, just a mile at a time at first.

One day he texted me: "ran 3 miles pops. lifted weights and did homework. luv ya."

We finally got an appointment to see a well-known pediatric orthopedic surgeon to discuss Leo's feet and the looming possibility of surgery. It had taken months to get scheduled with this specialist, who spent half an hour asking Leo about his life, about school, and then, after X-rays and a detailed exam, declared his feet to be "beautiful."

Yes, the condition he'd been diagnosed with was causing the fusion of a few bones. But many people live their entire life with that condition, the doctor explained. Some people don't even know they have it. He advised that stretching and running was a better plan than multiple surgeries. At least for now.

"I love your feet!" he said as Leo beamed.

20

Some nights it seemed Mary knew what we all needed: a sit-down family meal, one that required hours of chopping and prepping, getting the boys to set the table, washing lettuce, making salad dressing, pouring drinks—a meal that'd fill the house with warmth and aromas. She'd start early, slow-roasting a pork or simmering a meat sauce for hours.

One Saturday afternoon, as the boys slept well past noon, Mary and I started constructing such a feast—homemade pizzas, pasta with oxtail sauce, chicken and sausage for the grill, green beans and a salad. As dinnertime neared, Mary and I sipped our wine and she looked at all the platters of food and asked, "How many people are coming over again?"

The boys loitered in the kitchen and dining room, mocking my choice of music (Chet Baker, *Let's Get Lost*) and asking every five minutes, "When's dinner? I'm *hungry*."

We tried to get them to tell us about the previous night, and why they'd slept so late.

"Why are you so suspicious?" Sean asked Mary.

"Because I'm one-eighth Sicilian, that's why," Mary said.

Leo said he was sleeping at a girl's house that night— just messing with us, really—and Mary insisted on calling the girl's parents. "Here's what I need: address, home phone number, last name . . ." When Leo started waffling, Mary added: "I'm not going to call. But at least I'll know where to find you if aliens invade."

Getting bored, the boys began their ritual . . .

"Dude, I'm so gonna beat your ass," said Sean.

"I really wish you would try, dawg," said Leo, strapping on a Björn Borg–like headband: "I'll push you down the freakin' stairs."

"Do not come near me," Sean said, pulling on his boxing gloves and adopting a Russian-ish accent. "You do not want to fight me, my friend."

So it began . . .

"Ow, bro, stop. STOP! I didn't even hit you."

"Get off me, bro, your breath smells like poop."

"Calm down, dude. I barely touched you."

"Stop, stop, stop, stop, STOP! Ahhhh!"

"Oh, it's like that, huh? How's *this* smell? And *this*?"

"Ow, ow, ow—oh my god, bro, stop. Get off me. You're gonna break my fuckin' arm."

"No, I'm not—*you're* gonna break your arm. Stop resisting. You're like a wild animal."

"Your breath smells like *poop*!"

. . . a version of the same dialogue I'd been hearing for a dozen years.

During a previous battle, Mary had asked one of their friends, "Nathan, do you feel sorry for them? Is that why you hang out with them?"

Sean looked up from the floor, where he was entangled with Leo, and said, "He gets community service hours for hanging with us."

As always, the punching and shouting all came to a sudden halt when dinner was served.

The boys knew how much Mary valued our family meals. They were a staple of our family life, an enforced togetherness session, even if we sometimes had to pretend two of us at the table weren't a little stoned, and the other two weren't a little buzzed. Still, Mary had her table rules . . . If I tried to turn the stereo up, she'd turn it back down. If I tried to talk about things that didn't belong at the dinner table—homework, school, jobs—Mary would give me her "cool it" look. *Not now.*

And if the boys ever tried to skip a preplanned Saturday or Sunday night dinner, Mary would scold them, "You need to be part of the household *community.*" Once, when both boys blew us off for a big meal, Mary was despondent: "I'm not even a *mother* anymore. Who am I?"

Tonight, dinner complete, the table jammed with plates and bowls and bones, the four of us sat and talked for an hour, mostly about last night's teen adventures. We heard about them running into a skate friend who was back from rehab, had a job, an apartment, a girlfriend, a secondhand Cadillac. We heard about Sean's epic night celebrating a friend's birthday, moving the party and the mini keg from spot to spot as they got flushed out by police. They ended the night at a twenty-four-hour diner on Aurora Avenue, eating twelve-egg omelets as a parade of short-skirted prostitutes came through for coffees. "Some of them had Adam's apples," Sean reported.

Leo left the table to take a call on the front porch, then came back and whispered something to Sean. The two of them laughed, then launched into a refrain from a rap song, the meaning of which I didn't understand. They clearly had another big night planned. "Just call me Swayze," Leo announced. "Cuz I'm about to be *ghost*."

Mary and I exchanged looks, and I thought: this is so weird and wonderful. We're together. A funky union of four. I loved them so much. I loved *us* so much.

Nights like tonight, after a drawn-out dinner, the four of us for an hour or so, I'd be reminded that they still belonged to us. I'd reach out to touch them, hug them, muss their hair, punch an arm, grab them in a headlock. They'd resist a little—"get off me, *Dad*"—but without much bite, as if they needed it, too, some physical reminder that they were loved.

So many nights I'd torture myself with visions of harm, of annihilation. But tonight? With my boys at home, at least for now, all felt safer, *whole*. I could protect them because I could see them, hear them, touch them. I could be sure they were okay because they were enclosed by these walls, inside this home we'd built around us, our cocoon.

It won't last. It *can't*. It won't even last the night.

But at least for now, for this one true moment, our boys aren't on skateboards or in cars, they're here, home, ours.

Hours later, I stood brushing my teeth, thinking back on the day, lost in a dopey daze.

Mary and I had gone stand-up paddleboarding that morning. Out on Puget Sound, curious sea lions popped up their heads as we weaved among sailboats and trawlers and almost toppled in the wake of a container ship. We came home suntinged and sore, had a cocktail, started prepping our big dinner. And now it was bedtime. As toothpaste dribbled down my chin I heard clapping outside. I looked out the window down onto the driveway and saw Sean, applauding slow and sarcastic.

"Want me to do my bathroom dance for you?" I yelled.

He laughed. He was bathed in the floodlight, standing in the same spot where I'd watched him and Leo smoke a bowl a year earlier, then furiously kicked a hole in Sean's bedroom door. That pissed-off night, and others like it, seemed to be bobbing in our wake, at least for now. Sean had been doing construction work, saving money for a summer trip abroad. He was sunburned, wiry, and smiley—and sober? He looked like a young man.

"Get up here, *punk*," I called down.

Standing beside me, reflected in the bathroom mirror, my son was almost as tall as me. With his sticking-up hair, he seemed an inch taller. Skinny, pimply, handsome.

As I settled into bed with a book beside Mary, Sean joined us in our room, playing with Mickey and telling us about an after-dinner skate session with his boys.

Then we heard Leo come in . . . "Up here, Leo!"

Leo had been skating, too—the first time in months that his feet and ankles felt good enough. He described how strange it was to flub tricks that once came naturally, to go through the motions but wipe out. He wasn't sad about it, though—at least he was able to skate again.

I realized that we'd all been on boards that day. That'd probably never happened before. My body still sensed the rock and roll of the swells. My legs ached a little from trying to stay balanced and my arms hummed from paddling. I felt so good and didn't want the moment to end. "You can't go until you tell Mom and me a bedtime story," I said.

They rolled their eyes—"c'mon, *Dad*"—but I got the sense they didn't want to leave, either. Sean went first.

"Okay, you want a story? There was this kid named Crandall. And he dug a ditch for seven hours straight and then he died. Now that's a story."

"No, no, no," I said. "The story's gotta be at least a minute long and it can't end in death."

"Fine," Sean said. "There's this kid named Crandall, and he had to dig a ditch . . ."

I can't recall the rest, but he had me and Mary laughing as Leo heckled, poking holes in the story.

"And what's the moral of the story?" I asked when he finished.

"The moral? Does every story have to have a *moral?*" he

said, making air quotes, but he knew what I wanted. "All right, all right . . . the *moral* is that persistence pays off. *Okay?*"

Then it was Leo's turn, and he was ready for it. He launched into an elaborate tale of a kid who lived in a field full of dandelions, and every day he'd pluck one of the spent flowers and make a wish and blow away the wispy seeds. Day after day, he wished for tokens of wealth, a purple Mercedes, a helicopter, a yacht . . . I think he became a wealthy rapper in the end.

After Leo wrapped up his story, the boys decided to head downstairs to make ramen noodles and watch TV, but not before hugs and smart-ass devotions . . .

"I freakin' love you so much it hurts," said Leo.

"I love you as much as you need me to love you," said Sean.

I heard them clanging and arguing in the kitchen. I knew they'd probably stay up late watching their favorite shows for and about dumb-ass boys, *Workaholics*, *It's Always Sunny in Philadelphia*, *Trailer Park Boys*, or their go-to movie, *Step Brothers*.

My sons. They've remained so close, best friends, a team. They protect and respect each other. Even at seventeen and eighteen, they unselfconsciously embrace one another, tell each other "I love you." And that, I realized, has saved us. We love each other, we say it, we *mean* it. No matter what we've endured that day, as teens or adults, we rarely end a night in anger, without a hug. We'd become experts in reconciliation, in the art of hugs and I'm sorrys and I love yous.

I looked at the clock.

"Mary, it's only ten forty-five."

"I know. What's going on?"

"I don't know, but this is what I wished for . . . tonight . . . This is my dandelion wish."

My boys were home.

I could still feel those waves beneath my board, up and down, up and down, and it lulled me off to sleep.

EPILOGUE

HOME. ROOMS.

To look deep into your child's eyes and see in him both
yourself and something utterly strange, and then to
develop a zealous attachment to every aspect of him,
is to achieve parenthood's self-regarding yet unselfish
abandon.

—Andrew Solomon, *Far from the Tree*

'm opening paint cans and spreading tarps as Sean sleeps
deep and teen-like on his futon.

He's lightly snoring, a shirtless tangle of scrawny arms,
bruised and bony legs, a thrash of greasy hair, a sheen of
sweat across a dark-fuzz lip, my little dude on the edge of
manhood. As I always do when I watch him sleep, I flash

back to that hospital room, Sean tethered to monitors and Mary asleep in a foggy slump beside him. In the dozen years since, hardly a day has passed without my thinking how close we came to losing him. Would he always be that broken six-year-old boy to me?

We'd decided it was finally time to paint over his graffiti. Yesterday Sean made the ceremonial first roller swaths across bubble-fonted *Aztecs*. Today I'll finish the job.

I'll also replace the shredded door that I'd kicked through. And I'll trash Sean's defaced closet doors, the sliding panels that look like a 1970s New York City subway car. I look around at these walls and doors blanketed by graffiti, hidden scribbles from friends, assorted non sequiturs: "Stay dipped in butta," "Lorax," "pimp juice," "I hate boredom," "poop!" My gaze finds the 1970s wooden skateboard propped on a shelf, a gift from a friend during our cross-country skate trip, a Hobie model just like my first board.

Lately I've found myself lingering on the contents of my boys' rooms, items I'd overlooked during my drug-bust searches. Sure, I keep looking for house rules violations, a self-flagellating habit. But my heart's not in it as much. Sometimes I feel like an ER doctor, anticipating the next gunshot victim, in perpetual triage mode, unable to be just a laid-back family doc.

I sift through Sean's bookcase, through books and notebooks, finding bus passes, birthday cards, skate photos, including one of my favorites, a shot of Leo and Sean in midair, holding hands in a tandem kickflip off the top of a three-stair. They're flying. And I think: it's all gone by so fucking fast.

I turn on KEXP and listen to the Saturday reggae show, stirring my paint. I hate reggae, but today it feels appropriate. Sean keeps snoozing as I paint over one Aztec tag after another, and in no time I've got one wall covered in safe, soothing beige. I feel giddy, like something has shifted. That morning I'd read the *New York Times* coverage of the Supreme Court ruling on same-sex marriage, and I mooned over the explosion of rainbows on my Facebook and Twitter feeds. Today feels like a day of inclusion, tolerance, togetherness.

I take a coffee break, and something pulls me up to Leo's room. He's also still asleep, a question mark curl beneath his blanket. Instead of snooping through drawers I start scanning his walls, too.

A tiny Inner Space T-shirt hangs above his bed, signed by pro skaters from one of our first Seattle skate events. A "Sk8 the St8s" deck hangs beside a board with a photo of a lion eating its prey, designed by a cousin's friend who was killed while skating through downtown Chicago. Atop stereo speakers sit a pair of Independent trucks, a gift from Michael before he died. An orthopedic boot leans in a corner beside a graffiti-covered bookshelf crammed with stacks of skate magazines, a collection of snap-back caps, favorite skate shoes, and a few books. Skate stickers and Acres tags cover the desk and dresser, and the posters spread across the walls tell a story of boyhood aspirations—Big Lebowski,

Biggie Smalls, James Bond, Times Square, Muhammad Ali, plus a half dozen pro skaters in action. Tacked above his pillow is the dream catcher he made during summer camp a decade ago—the same summer he made me two T-shirts; one said TIGHT, the other said CRAP.

This weird inventory, this evidence of a life, of a skate boy's life, of my child's childhood . . . I realize these memorials of all things Leo won't hang here forever. My little man, one of my three best friends . . . this won't be his home much longer. I'm mostly okay with that. I'm happy for him. I'm girding myself for his moving-on-up . . .

As I quietly close the door I catch Bob Marley's eye, staring out from a poster above the quote that reads, "When you smoke the herb, it reveals you to yourself."

Let's hope so.

D ays later, I drop Sean at the airport and drive toward work when KEXP's morning DJ spins David Bowie, singing about these children, trying to change their world, immune to our consultations—*quite aware of what they're going through*. I try to sing along—*Ch-ch-ch-changes*—but out of nowhere the song grabs me by the throat. I choke up, and then I'm crying (*again*), and I have to pull over because I can't see a fucking thing.

My eldest is headed overseas, to spend the summer working and traveling through Spain. We've never been so far apart.

And it's only just beginning. A month after his Spain trip, Sean will fly back to Europe with Max and another friend to skateboard through Amsterdam, Prague, and Berlin. Nine months after that, Leo will launch his own European summer adventure, touring with a friend from Amsterdam to Prague, Greece, Croatia, Italy, Germany.

And just like that . . . our little Peter Pans are out past the borders of Neverland, out in the world, Lost Boys on their way to becoming men, becoming themselves.

I assumed I'd be ready, even eager, to set them free. But now? Who will I even *be* without my boys? Without being immersed in the daily churn of their chaotic existence?

We gave them so much freedom, hoping they'd learn what to do with it, hoping they'd get some things out of their system. It wasn't always pretty, but we stuck by them, stuck *with* them, and we emerged on the other side of it all, messy and loving, battle-hardened and intact.

Some nights I celebrate the weirdness of who we are, convinced that the skating, the street smarts, the travel, and the independence are the muddled ingredients of an exuberant life.

Other nights I worry for them, for their future. I try to keep it to myself, careful to protect their spirit, their late-teens vulnerability.

I'd long believed that skating had prepared them for the streets, for the out-of-bounds places, for the shadowy edges. But for the *real* world? During their tenuous exits from high school, I'd noticed something new. My sons, who rarely exhibited fear or caution, seemed tentative and unsure. They were outsiders emerging from the bubble they'd created into the world they'd avoided. From the fringe world they understood and controlled into the mainstream, a place that's scary and new, rigid and full of rules and expectations.

Watching them stand at the edge of their lives, suddenly hesitant and sensitive . . . I realize I've done all I can do.

But I want to give them one last nudge. I just want to tell them . . . You're doing great, boys. You're amazing.

Just lean forward. Just drop in.

ACKNOWLEDGMENTS

Friends and family who read shitty snippets and messy drafts, and/or offered advice, support, cocktails: David Shields, Peter Heller, Claire Dederer, Dani Shapiro, Brigid Schulte, Jennifer Senior, Tree Swenson, Jan and Laura Breuckner, Denise Kiernan, Joe D'Agnese, Elliot Reed, Lou King, Reid Adams, Blaise Schroeder, Don Ryan, Andrew Chapman, and Neal Bascomb.

Parents who shared their time, their memories, and allowed me to write about their complicated and amazing boys: Clark and Julie, Mario and Eve, Paul and Jen, Grimes and Brenda, Lou and Tina. Also Karen Colangelo, Marshall Stack Reid, and the crew from Inner Space.

Kickstarter supporters whose donations fueled the road trip that was the impetus for this book. (Here, many years later, is your thank-you prize.) A bonus shoutout to Lou and Reid for being part of the adventure. Also Adam Wiener.

Places to write and/or drink: Wellstone Center (thanks Steve), Whiteley Center (thanks Kathy), the Ace Hotel (NYC & L.A.), Wheelhouse Coffee (RIP), Assembly Hall, Uptown Espresso, Bauhaus Coffee, Picolinos, Java Bean, Walter's Scoop, Kings Hardware, Seattle ferries, Amtrak.

For inspiration and moral support: my colleagues, fellow writers, and readers at Amazon, Goodreads, and Audible; and the many partners I've befriended in the vital literary nonprofit community via the Amazon Literary Partnership.

At Ecco and HarperCollins: I can't say enough about the support, diligence, and care this book received from Dan Halpern, Miriam Parker, and, especially, my editor, Zack Wagman; big thanks to Martin Wilson, Sonya Cheuse, Andy LeCount, Ashley Mihlebach, Kristin Bowers, Meghan Deans, Ashley Garland, and others who helped bring this book to life, including Emma Janaskie, Allison Saltzman, Michelle Crowe, David Palmer, Shelly Perron, Victor Hendrickson, plus Megan Lynch and Michael Morrison.

To my agent and friend, Rob Weisbach, thanks for believing in this story every uncertain step of the way, and for always being there.

Huge, heartfelt, "hella" shoutouts to the young men who let me tell a piece of their story: Willem, Nate, Max, Nick, Nathan, Niall, and others.

Special thanks to my father, Phil, aka Jughead, and to my bold and crazy brother, Jeff.

And to Mary and my boys . . . I love you so.

RELATED READING

Barbarian Days: A Surfing Life by William Finnegan

This Boy's Life by Tobias Wolff

Lit, Cherry, The Liars' Club, and *The Art of Memoir*
by Mary Karr

The Night of the Gun by David Carr

Slow Motion, Still Writing, and *Hourglass* by Dani Shapiro

Townie by Andre Dubus III

Poser and *Love and Trouble* by Claire Dederer

All Joy and No Fun by Jennifer Senior

Weed the People by Bruce Barcott

Manhood for Amateurs by Michael Chabon

Live Through This by Debra Gwartney

Kook by Peter Heller

Beautiful Boy by David Sheff

Wild by Cheryl Strayed

The Tender Bar by J. R. Moehringer

Eat, Pray, Love by Elizabeth Gilbert

Overwhelmed by Brigid Schulte

Half a Life by Darin Strauss

The Book of Men: Eighty Writers on How to Be a Man, curated by Colum McCann

Indignation by Philip Roth

When I First Held You: 22 Critically Acclaimed Writers Talk About the Triumphs, Challenges, and Transformative Experience of Fatherhood, edited by Brian Gresko

By Tony Hawk: *Hawk: Occupation Skateboarder; How Did I Get Here? The Ascent of an Unlikely CEO*

Impossible: Rodney Mullen, Ryan Sheckler, and the Fantastic History of Skateboarding by Cole Louison

The Answer Is Never: A Skateboarder's History of the World by Jocko Weyland

The Great Floodgates of the Wonderworld by Justin Hocking

Life & Limb: Skateboarders Write from the Deep End, edited by Justin Hocking, Jeff Knutson, and Jared Jacang Maher

Hosoi: My Life as a Skateboarder Junkie Inmate Pastor by Christian Hosoi